# OXHEY
IN PICTURES

# CHARTER OF OXHEY
## AD 1007

### As translated by Reverend Newton Price 1897

*"In the everlasting Kingdom of GOD and Our Lord Jesus Christ.* – The merits of the blessed martyrs throughout the world should indeed be extolled with divine praises; and the prayers of those who shed their blood for the name of Christ should be invoked with all earnestness, but specially the glorious victory of the blessed martyr Alban should be honoured by the English tribes dwelling within the limits of Britain; for he endured martyrdom for Christ, and also consecrated this nation by the outpouring of his life blood. Wherefore I Æthelred, by the grace of GOD, King of all Albion, in order that on the awful day of Judgment I may by the intercession of the saints be deemed worthy to be admitted coheir of the heavenly kingdom, do give to Almighty GOD the possession of three lands to be held for ever for the monastery of the aforesaid martyr. Of which lands two lie side by side: i.e., one at *North-tun* and one at *Rodanhangra*; but the third lies apart from the others and is commonly called at *Oxangehæge*. Of these lands Offa, king of the Mercians, formerly held a part in right of his kingdom, and granted it for ever, and free from all conditions, to the before named monastery, for the love of the great martyr who rests there. But after his death this part was seized against all right by wicked men who were in power – and for a time was unjustly severed from that monastery, until at length it came into the possession of the Earl Leofsige. And when he for his offence was sent into banishment, Ælfric, my faithful Archbishop, and the Abbot Leofric his brother, by my permission having paid the price purchased the said portion. And they further obtained by petition of their humble devotion that I should restore to GOD what was GOD'S. But after the death of the before named Archbishop, at the intercession of his brother, I gave command to write this charter of my gift and renewal, in which I ordain by my own authority and that of Almighty GOD, that no one, be he high or low, of what rank soever, presume under any pretence to deprive the holy martyr of this possession, either in my own reign or in the time of my successors; but that this grant of restitution stand and be valid for ever, and all attempts of opposing parties be made void. And the possession of the said lands shall be held gifted with the same liberty as the aforesaid King of the Mercians endowed with all devotion the Monastery of Saint Alban and all the property which he granted to that body, three services excepted: proportionate contribution to the army, and the repairing of bridges and fortresses. But all things belonging to these estates, as fields, pastures, meadows, woods and the rest shall remain free. If any one therefore shall presume to break these ordinances, let him have no part in the blessing of Almighty GOD and of all the Saints, and of me and of all Christian people, and let him perish condemned with eternal malediction, unless he speedily set right that in respect of which he has sinned against GOD and His holy Martyr Alban."

"These are the boundaries of Oxangehæge and Bæcceswyrth. First from Watford into Pudawyrth. Thence into Mapuldorgeat. Thence to East Heal to the three boundaries. Thence to the Crucifix.

Thence to the Small Oak. Thence to the Hoar Thorn. Thence to the Defe. Thence to Beorclege. Thence to Cuthhelming Tree. Thence to the Stile. Thence to R….dng Well. Thence to Colne Bridge."

I Æthelred, King of the English, for the love of GOD and the holy martyr Albans, gladly renew this gift.
I Ælfeah, Archbishop of Canterbury, place the sign of the Holy Cross, in confirmation of this royal gift.
I Ælfgifu, the Queen, consent with a devout mind.
I Wulfstan, Archbishop of York, give my consent to this assignment.
I Æthelstan, son of the King, with my brothers, approve.
I Athelwold, Bishop of Winchester, assent.
I Ordbyrht, Bishop of the South Saxons, confirm this deed.

*The names of the following Bishops are also attached:* Adulf, Lyving, Godwine, Ælfgar, with the other Bishops. *Then follow the names of eleven Abbots:* Ælfsige *(three times),* Ælfweard, Wulfgar, Germanus Ælfere, Birhtwold, Ælfmær, Eadnoth, and Godeman. *After these are two Earls,* Ælfric, Leofwine, *and sixteen Thanes, viz.,* Eadric, Ælfgar *(twice),* Æthelmær, Athelwold *(twice),* Leofwine *(twice),* Godric, Æthelwine *(twice),* Byrhsige, Ulfkytel, Æthelric, Oswig, Ælfwig.

*The following is a translation of the endorsement, which is in the same hand in which the Charter is written:* "This is the Charter of the three estates, Northtun, Rodanhangra, and Oxangehæge, with Bæcceswyrth; which estates Ælfric, Archbishop, and his brother Leofric, Abbot, bought. And Æthelred, the King, then assigned them by charter to S.Alban's Monastery, in everlasting inheritance for the service of Almighty God."

# OXHEY
IN PICTURES

Compiled by
Christine Cooling
and Ian Mackay

Published by
Oxhey Village Environment Group

First published 2000

© Copyright C. M. Cooling & I. R. Mackay

© Copyright of pictures and illustration remain with the owners

All rights reserved. Except for any fair dealing for the purposes of research or private study,
no part of this publication may be reproduced, stored or transmitted, in any form or by any means,
electrical, mechanical, photocopying or otherwise without permission of the authors.

Published by Oxhey Village Environment Group

29 Avenue Terrace, Oxhey, Watford WD19 4AP

ISBN 0-9539685-0-2

Typesetting & layout by John Fearnside

Scanning by John Fearnside, John Purkis & Bryan Hutt

Printed by Admin Press (Watford) Ltd

538 Whippendell Rd, Watford

Bushey Arches C1900

OXHEY IN PICTURES

# Contents

| | |
|---|---|
| Frontispiece: Oxhey Charter A.D. 1007 | ii |
| Foreword | 2 |
| Acknowledgements | 3 |
| Ode to Oxhey! | 4 |
| Chapter 1: Oxhey's Origins | 5 |
| Chapter 2: Oxhey Scenes | 15 |
| Chapter 3: Oxhey's Buildings | 49 |
| Chapter 4: Transport | 79 |
| Chapter 5: People and Events | 95 |
| Information on OVEG and address for ordering copies of this book | 122 |
| Bibliography | 123 |

Cover picture: 14 Chalk Hill – Grade II Listed Building (courtesy of Alan Luto).

OXHEY IN PICTURES

## ❧ Foreword ❧

The Oxhey Village Environment Group was formed in 1975 with the objectives of preserving the character of Oxhey Village, fostering its community spirit and recording the history of life in its area. So this book draws on 25 years of patient collection of shared memories and photographs. The Millennium seemed an appropriate opportunity to publish a selection of these for the benefit of present and future inhabitants of Oxhey and also for anyone who is interested in the origins and development of what we have now come to regard as an 'urban village'.

This collection was not produced simply as a journey into rose-tinted nostalgia – the houses and buildings depicted were usually cold and damp, the roads muddy, rutted and dangerous, the steam trains a source of noise and dirt and many of the people usually hungry. Living in Oxhey today is easier and more comfortable for most of us but it may be that, almost as a consequence of this, we are now in danger of damaging the fragile character of our district. It is important that we are aware of what has gone before. History – like life – is a process of constant adjustment to change. When changes are proposed to our environment they should be assessed from a knowledge of what has gone before so that we are able to protect that which is of value from the past. Although Oxhey's four most prestigious buildings are protected by their 'Listing' and our major open spaces by the Green Belt the character of the area depends on the more modest homes and their gardens whose groupings may carry quite as much history as the 'Stately Home'.

It is hoped that OVEG's book will contribute to solving the dilemma of achieving a satisfactory balance between conservation and future development and, possibly, encourage others to research further into the history of the Oxhey area. We hope you will get as much fun from 'finding out' as we have.

C. C. & I. M.

## ~ Acknowledgements ~

The pictures in this book have been selected from many sources. Our thanks are due to all those who have scoured their collections (and their lofts) and allowed us to copy their photos. Very special thanks are due to Bryen Wood of Bushey Museum both for his generosity in allowing us access to his collection of photographs and for his help and advice on the history of our district. We are grateful to the Watford Museum and Watford Reference Library for allowing us access to their photographic collections. Thanks are also due to the following for the use of their documents, photographs or expertise: Audrey Adams, Andy Billings, Coleen Devenish, Doreen Doe, James Gatesman, Neil Hamilton, Geoff Harris, Doreen Hinds, Bryan Hutt, Jill Ibbott, Frances Jaggard, Alan Luto, Vicky Mackay, Ray Penrose, Mary Reid, Marjorie Richards, Norman Salmon, Cyril Sheldrake and Leslie Smith. We are indebted to John Liffen, Graham Rhodda and Doug Rose for the detailed particulars of the trains featured in Chapter 4. Sadly, we are unable, owing to lack of space, to thank everyone who has helped individually but we hope that you will understand and forgive and will be pleased to have contributed to the production of OVEG's 'Oxhey in Pictures'. In compiling the historical notes and captions we have used information gleaned from books, newspaper reports and, importantly, the memories of local people. Please excuse and, where possible, let us know of any errors which may have crept in. We accept responsibility for these and will aim to correct them in any later collections which OVEG may publish.

We also acknowledge, with gratitude, grants from Watford Borough Council, Hertsmere Borough Council and Herts County Council which have made possible the printing of this collection.

C. C. & I. M.

Any proceeds from the sale of this book will be given to local charities or towards local group projects.

OXHEY IN PICTURES

# Ode to Oxhey!

Where is Oxhey? We cannot quite tell
It's up on the Hill and it's down in the Dell
   Next to high Arches with trains rattling by
It's Woods and 'swallow holes' where mysteries lie.

   It's somewhere 'twixt Bushey and old Watford town
Then south-west and a bit further down,
   It marks where London halts its spread,
It touches the Colne's willow-lined bed.

   It's an empty Reservoir 'neath grassy mound,
A Village Green, once a brick field ground.
   It's a Heath with a Cross to those who fell,
It's shops, it's Allotments, an Orchard as well.

   It's Victorian terrace and semi-detached,
Oxhey's Chapel ancient, unmatched,
   It's roads that are narrow and twist on their way
- Wholely unsuited to traffic today.

   T'was cottages for workers on rail, mills or clay
Which now house commuters to London each day.
   We may not be 'scenic', we've slowly evolved
But the secret of Oxhey is easily solved –

   For young and old it's a home that we love
An heirloom to guard against threats from 'above'
   So the story in pictures of Oxhey's past ages
We display for your pleasure in t'following pages!

                                  I. M., B. H. & C. C.

## Chapter 1

# Oxhey's Origins

TO UNDERSTAND THE landscape of the Oxhey area it is only natural to start with the underlying geology which controls its physical features. Chalk underlies the whole area but most of this is obscured by the later Lambeth Series and by drift deposits of ancestral Thames terrace gravels and pebble beds. Chalk outcrops at the surface only occasionally, as at Chalk Hill. The mainly clayey Lambeth Series usually form the lower ground. However where these are protected by caps of gravel or pebble beds, which are more resistant to erosion, higher ground such as Reservoir Hill and Watford Heath results. It is the clays of the Lambeth Series and London Clay which gave rise to the many local brickworks which were important in the nineteenth century development of Oxhey. Lime kilns, based on the Chalk of Chalk Hill, also utilised a local raw material.

The earliest traces of human activity found locally date from Stone and Iron Age times. It is thought that the Roman Akeman St may have run near the line now followed by Chalk Hill and the London Rd. The first official mention of Oxhey by name is in the eighth century when King Offa gave Oxangehæge to the Benedictine Abbey of St Albans.

Typical clay landscape with Attenborough's Fields, Margeholes Wood and Oxhey Lane. Oxhey Grange is in the foreground with Elm Avenue on the left. The hedge running diagonally across the picture marks the parish boundary. 1994.

The pattern of early settlement and later development of Oxhey was influenced not only by its soils but also by its geographical position. Its proximity to the road north from London and its contacts with St Albans Abbey would have been important early influences. By the end of the nineteenth century, however, it was the arrival of the railway and the fast developing town of Watford, which absorbed Oxhey in due course, that had become dominant factors in Oxhey's growth.

The following maps trace Oxhey's development during the past three centuries from an essentially rural landscape based on manor-house estates with their dependent hamlets and surrounded by fields and woodlands. After the arrival of the railway in the late 1830s the pattern of settlement changed dramatically, as shown in the maps of 1871 and 1890. Since then the district has become increasingly urbanised but Oxhey is fortunate in retaining some of its earlier rural character since parts of it extend within the protection of London's Green Belt.

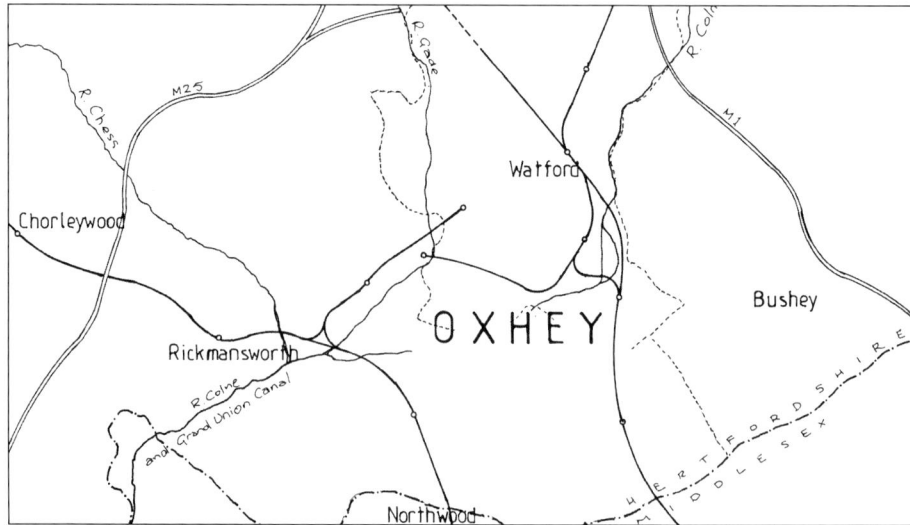

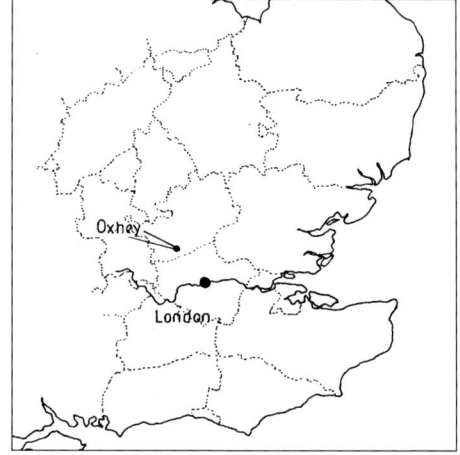

Location plans showing the position of Oxhey.

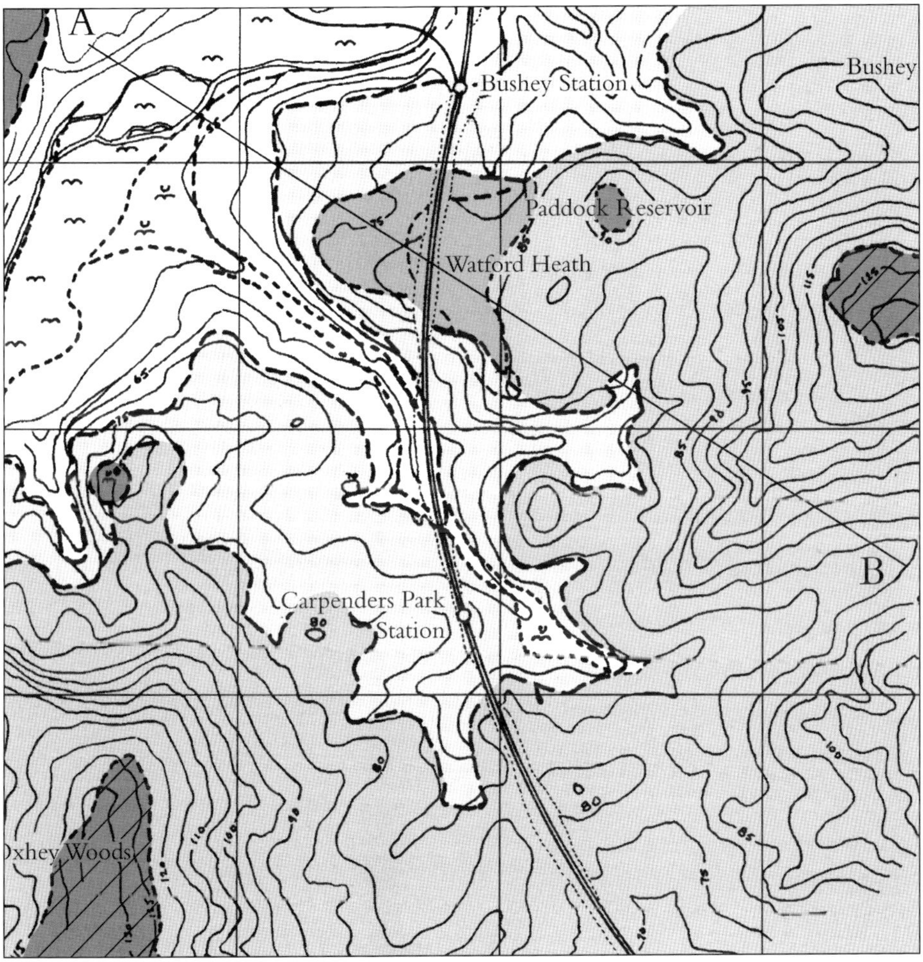

Physical features and geology of the Oxhey area.

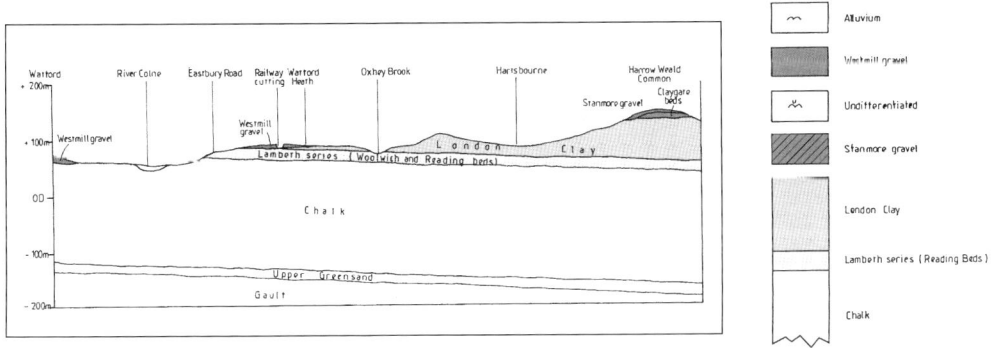

Geological section A-B.

OXHEY IN PICTURES

Dury & Andrews Map showing the Oxhey part of Watford Parish in 1766.

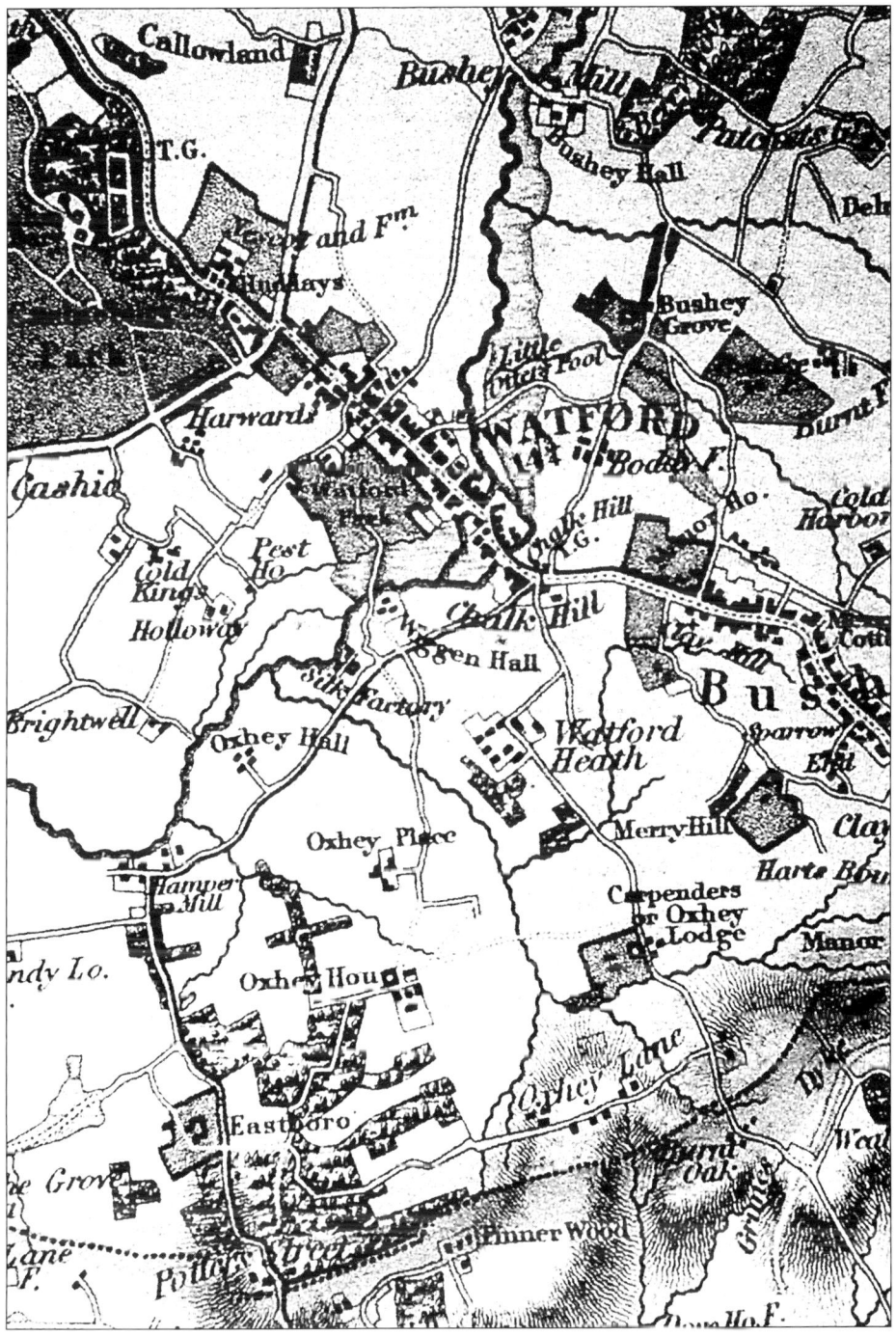

Part of Crutchley's map of the environs of London, 1824.

Map of Oxhey district, 1871.

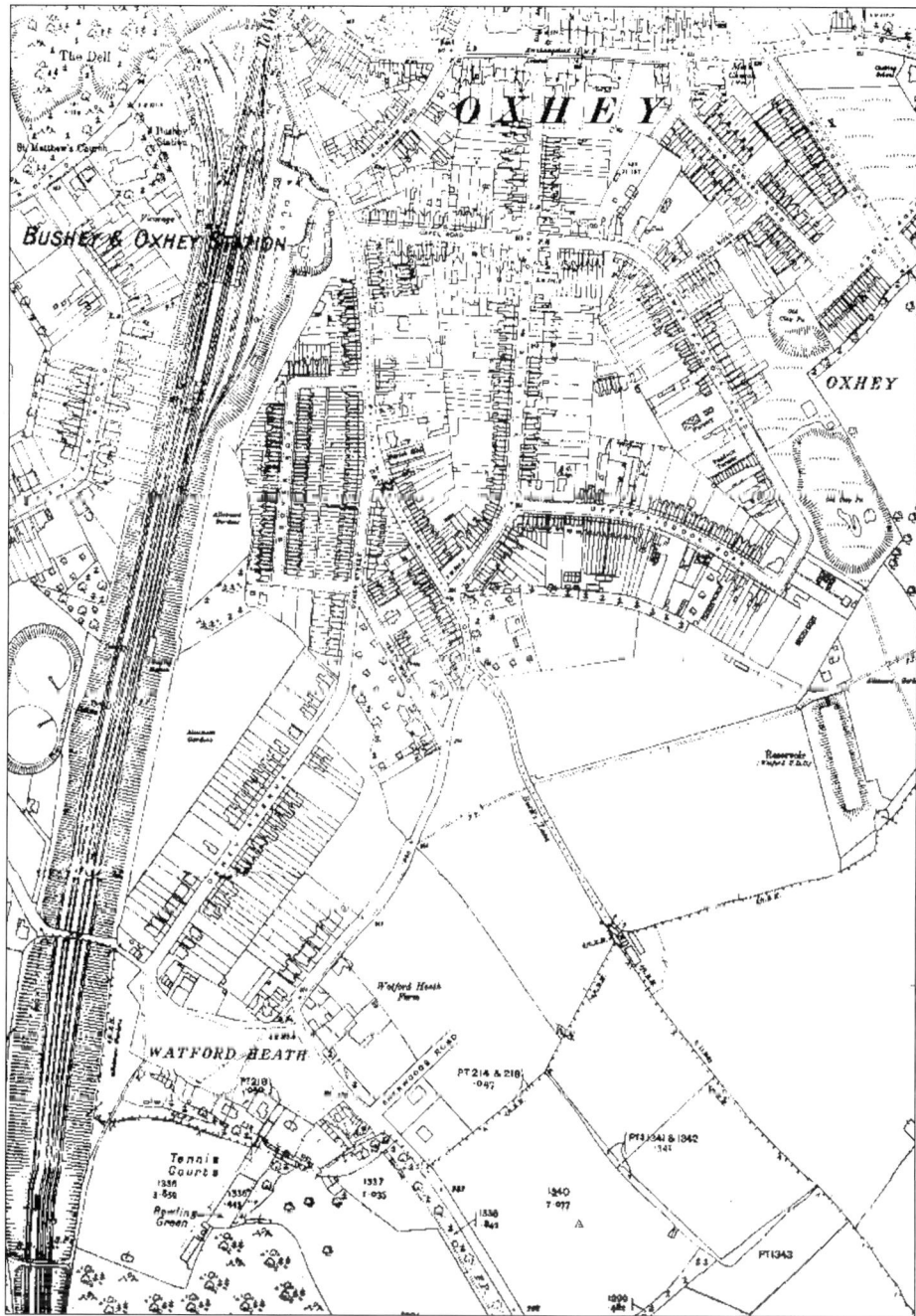

Oxhey, c1920 (part of a map included in the sales material for the Oxhey Grange estate sale, 1932).

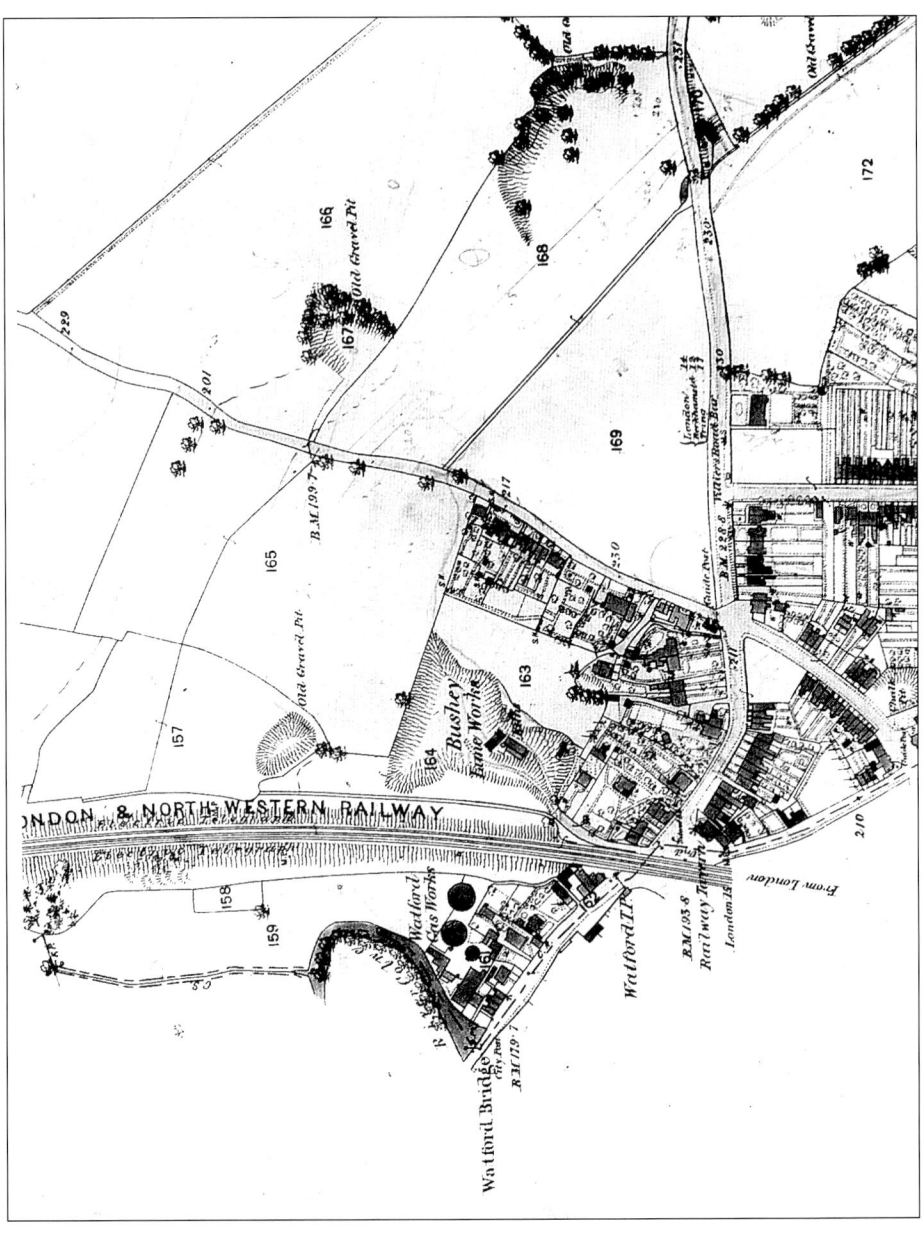

'New Bushey', Chalk Hill and the Railway, 1890.

Lime kilns near Bushey Arches on the north side of Chalk Hill. Local Chalk was burned in the kilns to provide lime for mortar, for plastering walls and as white-wash. It was also used as 'quick-lime' for spreading on fields to neutralise acid soils.

Henry Drake, who lived in Lime Kiln Cottage, with his family (L to R, Harry, Elsie, Daisy, George and Ada). Both Harry and George were killed in WW I.

Watford Heath Brickworks. Section showing the base of the London Clay overlying clays of the Lambeth Series. Watford Heath Brickworks were in Oxhey Lane opposite a part of Oxhey Grange estate.

Artist's impression of the various activities being carried out on the Paddock Brick Field (now restored as Oxhey Green), c1880.

## Chapter 2
# Oxhey Scenes

As OUR VERSE indicates, Oxhey suffers from something of an identity crisis – despite being able to trace its name from the time of King Offa (757-796 AD) who gave the district of Oxangehæge to the Benedictine Abbey of St Albans to which it was later restored in the Charter of 1007 (see frontispiece). The historic boundaries described in the Charter are now uncertain (although Bæcceswyrth is probably Batchworth) and have in any case changed since that time. The mansions, farms and features which have 'Oxhey' in their name may no longer be within the administrative limits of present day Oxhey. We have included several of these in our walk round Oxhey because they 'feel' like Oxhey – we apologise to anyone who considers their territory has been invaded and to others who feel arbitrarily excluded, we hope you will understand.

The 'views' of Oxhey reproduced in this Chapter are those which a walker – wandering both in time and space – would encounter on a stroll, starting in the south-west by Oxhey Woods and passing via Hampermill and Eastbury Rd to Green Lane and Oxhey Park, then up Pinner Rd to Watford Heath and on into Oxhey Village finishing, perhaps a little wearily, on a bench in Attenborough's Fields.

Cattle in Attenborough's Fields looking towards Cross Rd (1986).

Oxhey District Boundary Marker No 2; near the footbridge over Haydon Hill Pond.

Boundary Marker No 3; VW Garage, corner of London Rd & Vale Rd.

These Boundary Markers were set up in 1879 when the separate district and parish of Oxhey was created. BM No 1 is lost and its precise position uncertain but it was reputed to have been near the present kissing-gate between Attenborough's Fields and the Paddock Rd Allotments.

Boundary Marker No 4; outside 61 Aldenham Rd.

OXHEY IN PICTURES

View of Oxhey Woods, c1910.

Oxhey Woods, although smaller in extent, had changed little by the 1950s.

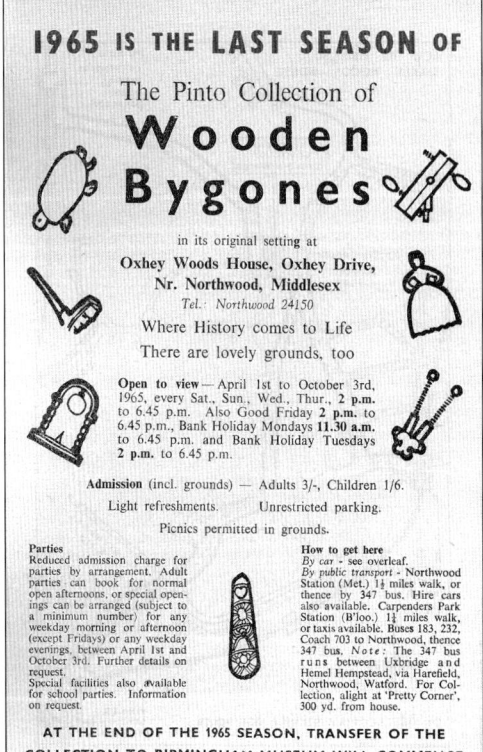

Oxhey Woods House, home of the Pinto Collection of Wooden Bygones. Mr & Mrs Pinto collected all manner of 'treen' (wooden articles of any sort, tools, equipment or ornaments) and displayed them in their home. The collection was open to the public and was a notable tourist attraction until 1965 when it was transferred to the Birmingham Museum of Science & Industry.

Poster for the Pinto Collection, 1965.

Evidence of an Iron Age settlement was found near Hampermill by Dr Davey of 61 Eastbury Rd in the nineteen twenties. This is certainly one of the oldest documented sites in Oxhey. A mill, probably on this site, was recorded in the Domesday Book and was likely to have been owned by St Albans Abbey, by 1356 it was referred to as Hamper Myll. At the Dissolution of the Monasteries (1536-39) the mill passed to George Zowche and was renamed Souche's Mill. By 1556, still a grain mill, it had reverted to being 'Hampermill'. It had become a paper mill by 1776 and was owned by a Mr Leopard. The mill was rebuilt in 1793 and high quality hand-made paper was manufactured up to c1908. It fell into disuse before 1930.

Hampermill in the snow before 1909.

The Colne at Hampermill.

General view of houses and buildings at Hampermill, early 1900s.

Hampermill c1900.

Eastbury Rd, before 1910, the roadway and footpaths are unsurfaced but gas street lighting has been installed.

Inter-war houses were built along Hampermill Lane overlooking fields and the River Colne. When the foundations for houses in Thorpe Crescent were dug Dr Davey discovered worked flint implements over 12,000 years old, the earliest evidence of settlement in the Oxhey area.

The 15th Green of Oxhey Golf Course, showing its notorious bunkers. Beyond, across the Eastbury Rd, is the Colne Valley Water Co's Eastbury Pumping Station built above a series of wells and headings in the Chalk to supply water to the rapidly expanding local population in the late 1920s.

Green Lane, when it was a private entrance to Oxhey Place, providing access for pedestrians and horsedrawn vehicles, c 1900.

Green Lane, near the stream before Brookdene Avenue was built.

Green Lane, before 1913.

Green Lane, looking south towards Oxhey Golf Course, 1930s.

Tommy Deacon's (now Deacon's) Hill c1915. For eight generations the eldest son of the Deacon family, who owned Wiggenhall and the land on either side of Deacon's Hill, including Oxhey Park, was named Thomas. Several local legends attach to 'Tommy' Deacon; the favourite says he rode down the hill for a bet, broke his neck and is buried in the 'greensward where four roads meet at the foot'; another says he lies near the summit. The Wiggenhall Estate was purchased by the local authority in 1920.

Old Wiggen Hall Bridge was the private property of Mr Blackwell, Watford was paying him £1 per annum for its use in 1907. The bridge was replaced in the 1920s.

Boat House owned by Richard Andrew-Arthur, at the foot of Tommy Deacon's Hill in the 1920s. A 'Mrs Deacon, who kept the "Fighting Cocks" by the side of the Colne, had two boats which were let for hire at a shilling an hour' in the late nineteenth century. Pleasure boats could still be hired into the 1930s.

The River Colne, Oxhey Park, looking towards Bushey Arches, 1930s.

River Colne, Oxhey Park, view towards Wiggenhall Bridge, 1950s.

Oxhey Park, view over the Colne towards Watford, c1950. The park keeper's lodge, demolished in the 1960s, is in the background. The Park, which formerly formed part of the Wiggenhall Estate, was formally opened in 1924.

## Oxhey in Pictures

A peaceful Pinner Rd, c1910, looking south from its junction with Capel Rd, only horse-drawn traffic in sight.

Pinner Rd, from the corner of Capel Rd, with Horne's (later Benton's) sweet shop and tobacconists (now Oxhey Angling Centre) on the corner, 1900s.

Capel Rd, with Caroline Place on the right near the figures, c1910. The cast iron 'bollard' (foreground right) was a London Coal Duties post bearing the City of London Shield and the inscription '24 Vict'. It was moved to New St, Watford in the 1960s and subsequently removed (for safe keeping?) by the Borough during the 'enhancement' work.

Grover Rd in the 1920s before the parking problem became acute.

FEATURES IN PINNER RD.
This statue of Queen Victoria, marking Queens Terrace, is fixed over the door of 37 Pinner Rd at the corner of Grover Rd.

The Victorian Post Box, dated 1881, and let into the side wall of the former Co-op at the junction of Pinner Rd and Oxhey Avenue was removed in the 1980s.

The polished pink Aberdeen Granite drinking fountain (c1882) on the island by Watford Heath was dedicated to the memory of William Eley of Oxhey Grange. It had chained metal drinking cups and, a thoughtful touch, a water trough for the dogs. The fountain was demolished by the Borough Council to make way for road improvements in 1959. Pieces are said to have made their way into local rockeries.

Looking from Watford Heath towards the old school, the 'new' houses in Pinner Rd and the drinking fountain, early 1900s.

Watford Heath looking towards Rose Tea Cottage.

Corner of Watford Heath showing mediæval cottages which formerly stood on the site of the present inter-war houses, (early 1920s). The two ponds on the Heath were filled in as a health hazard in 1908 using materials from the widening of Pinner Rd. They are thought to have been located near these cottages.

Watford Heath, 1920s, showing the War Memorial Cross.

Watford Heath, 1900s. Many of the original cottages were 'copyhold', an ancient form of land tenure which allowed the 'tenant' to pass on the property to his heirs so long as the dues continued to be paid to the land lord. Copyholders also had the right to vote in parliamentary elections up to the nineteenth century.

Watford Heath, late 1940s, showing the more recent half-timbered houses.

Rose Tea Cottage and Tea Garden, Watford Heath which is said to have been built by the Penroses of Oxhey Grange for a daughter who ran the tea rooms. The garden boasted an elaborate topiary hedge reading 'TEAS' which survived until the late 1940s. During WW II Miss Chapman had her school in the small hall on the right. This was also used for bible classes and private parties while Mr & Mrs Nelson Baker ran their confectioners shop on the left. It is now a private house.

# Oxhey in Pictures

Watford Heath from the east with the 'Wheatsheaf' inn sign and a notice promulgating the bylaws.

Watford Heath in 1940s, semi-detached houses, which replaced the mediæval cottages, in the distance. Grange Cottage is thought to have been built for the washerwoman who served Oxhey Grange. The ironing and airing was done in the building now called 'The Barn' at the rear.

Oxhey Lane in the 1890s? Looking towards Watford with Carpenders Avenue on the left.

Cows from Oxhey Lane Farm Dairy having won first and second prizes at the Watford Show in 1909.

Oxhey Lane, two cottages built by James Penrose, of Oxhey Grange, about 1918 near former Watford Heath brickfield (see page 14).

Oxhey Rd, over the railway bridge 1930s. The fence on the right overlooked the cutting and water troughs and was a great place for the train spotters of earlier generations.

Watford Heath Lodge and start of Oxhey Rd railway bridge, 1920s with Little Goblins Cottages, now demolished, beyond.

Oxhey Avenue 1950s. This 'new' development was built as a continuation of Oxhey St c1913. The two roads were 'merged' and all re-numbered 'Oxhey Avenue' in 1952.

Dorothy Wolfe near the former Caledonian Laundry in Oxhey St, 1904.

Group of school boys in Lower Paddock Rd. Oxhey Village, c1900.

Capel Rd (c1910s), shops included the Handy Stores and Luckett's dairy.

Capel Rd, the same shops 1999 before they were converted into houses and offices.

*Capell Road, Oxhey.*

Capel and Villiers Rd cross-roads, the Rifle Volunteer on the left hand corner, Palmers (grocers 1938-1996) opposite, Lovedays (bakers 1935-present, these premises have been a bakehouse since before 1910). The two-gabled building in the distance near St Matthews church steeple is Oxhey's former vicarage.

*Villiers Road, Oxhey.*

Villiers Rd looking towards the Baptist Church (1960s). Oxhey Post Office was double its present size, the chemists next door belonged first to Mr Gant (1930s), then Mr Dyson – at the time of this photo – and is now 'Bonds'.

King Edward Rd, near Warneford Place and looking towards Cross Rd. The Methodist's 'School Room' on the left was moved bodily from its site as the former Methodist Chapel at 45/45a Villiers Rd (see page 62). It was demolished in 1963 to make room for the new hall.

Junction of Villiers Rd with the London Rd looking east. The houses on the left were built and owned by the Benskin family of Benskin's Brewery Watford (c1910s).

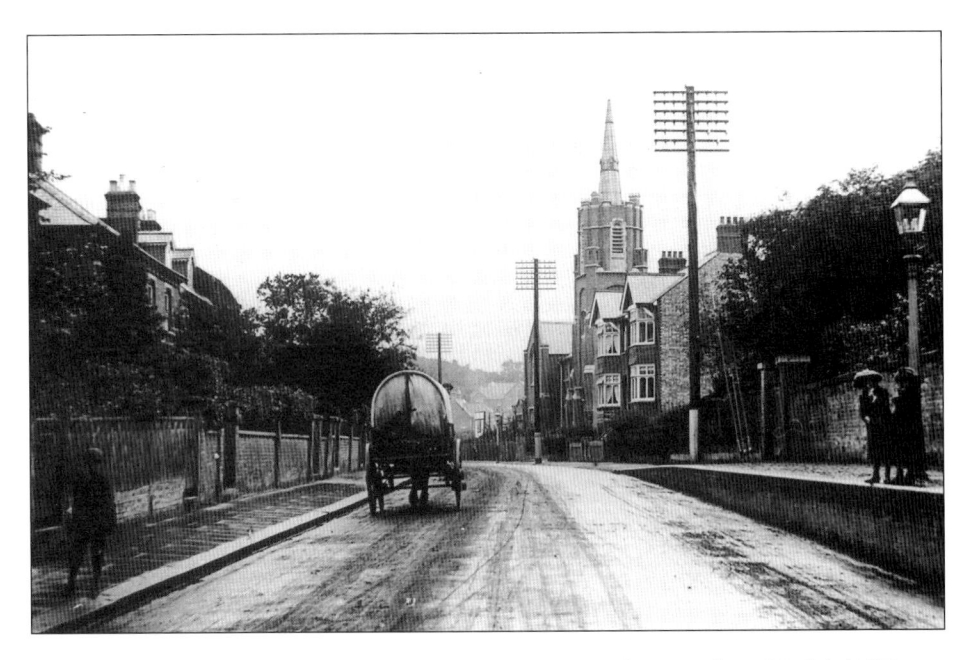

London Rd with the Methodist Church on the corner of King Edward Rd (c1915).

London Rd/Chalk Hill at cross-roads with Aldenham Rd; the Victoria on the right.

OXHEY IN PICTURES

The raised pavement on London Rd/Chalk Hill looking west towards Ye Corner.

View east up Chalk Hill with two way traffic, 1961.

OXHEY IN PICTURES

Chalk Hill/Aldenham Rd cross-roads. 'Ye Corner', named by its builder in the 1920s, with the Hygienic Dairy, later Lee, Wiggs & Clark. The archway just up the hill is the entrance and all that remains of a cinema which was never built owing to the outbreak of WW I. These premises currently house the tatooist. On the right is Oxhey Infants and Junior School on the site now occupied by Faithfield.

A rather romanticised picture of a snow covered Aldenham Rd, c1890.

## Oxhey in Pictures

View north-east up Aldenham Rd from the Oxhey Boundary Marker. Former Colne Valley Water Co offices on the left; Jaggard, Builders (now Rosewood Stores) on the right on the corner of Vale Rd.

The 'Reservoir', near Field End Close, actually a former covered pressure tank which supplied water by gravity to Watford. The grass covered slope facing Reservoir Cottage formerly had a wide flight of stone steps with a parapet on either side and a large 'hairpin-shaped' pipe arch at the top (1999).

Reservoir Cottage and its gauge house, opposite the 'Reservoir' (1986). 'The highest house in Oxhey'.

Talbot Avenue, a typical inter-war development built, with Wilcot Avenue, on Henderson Field by Grover & Higgs in the 1920s. A family outing – no cars only bicycles, 1945.

# Oxhey in Pictures

Paddock Rd Allotments, Park House and Oxhey Green in the middle distance with Watford and St Albans beyond (Painting by Ian Lyons, 1971).

Park House and garden, Upper Paddock Rd. Built by Joseph Foster, a former head gardener from Oxhey Grange, in 1867. In 1911 it was bought by Frederick King who started a nursery business. The nursery flourished following his return from the war in 1920 and he built seven glasshouses in which he raised his King's No1 and No2 tomatoes. The glasshouses were damaged by blast in WW II but the nursery continued on a smaller scale until he sold the land fronting Upper Paddock Rd to build Nos 85 & 87 in 1959.

47

Law's Nurseries, Lower Paddock Rd, c1940 (where Nos 81 to 87 now stand). Note brown paper strips stuck on the windows of the house opposite as protection against bomb blast.

Volunteers emplacing a bench in memory of Frank Marshall in Attenborough's Fields (1998). View towards St James Church, Bushey.

## Chapter 3

# Oxhey's Buildings

Most of Oxhey's buildings date either from the Victorian building boom or else the periods shortly after each of the two World Wars plus recent 1990s 'infill'. Few of the manor houses, which formerly characterised Oxhey, remain standing but the district can still boast the unique seventeenth century Oxhey Chapel and a timber-framed house at 14 Chalk Hill of the same date.

The following pictures mainly feature buildings which older Oxheyites will recollect; they have been grouped in the following order – historic houses, churches, schools and shops, finishing up with a 'pub crawl'.

Gates to Oxhey Grange; said to have been presented to Oliver Cromwell in 1649, subsequently removed from Dreyton Manor to Cassiobury House and thence to Oxhey Grange in the 1930s.

Oxhey Grange, 1925.

Garden at Oxhey Grange. This picture, featuring Mr & Mrs Penrose, was on their Christmas card for 1928.

The Penrose Family (c1882). James Doyle Penrose, on the far right aged about 20, was to occupy Oxhey Grange after the Eleys. Penrose was a Quaker and an artist of the 'Romantic School'. The Oxhey Grange estate was purchased from the Penroses by the Absaloms, who built the Carpenders Park estate, in 1932.

Particulars for the sale of Oxhey Grange in 1932.

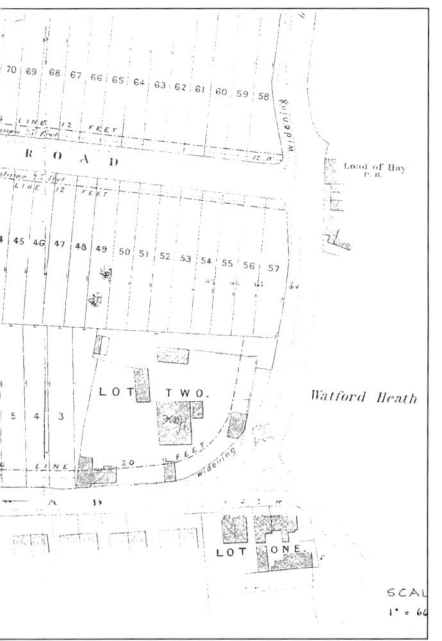

Two illustrations of Watford Heath Farm, demolished in the 1960s, now the site of flats of the same name.

Plan from the sales particulars of land for building plots in the triangle forming Pinner Rd, Sherwoods Rd and Bucks Avenue. 1914.

## Particulars.

### LOT 1.

# 5 Freehold brick-built & slated Cottages

KNOWN AS

## Nos. 1 to 5, WATFORD HEATH.

Nos. 1 and 2 each contain 2 Bedrooms, Sitting Room and Kitchen, and a timber and slated Coalshed and Washhouse, with copper and sink, and a W.C. outside; small gardens back and front. Let to Mr. N. Dilkes at 4/6 per week, and Mr. Baker at 5/6 per week respectively;

No. 3 contains 3 Bedrooms, Sitting Room and Kitchen combined, and Scullery; outside, W.C. and Coalshed. Let to Mr. B. Pamment at 4/6 per week.

No. 4 contains 3 Bedrooms, Sitting Room, Kitchen and Scullery; outside, W.C. and Coalshed. Let to Mr. W. Hatton at 7/6 per week.

No. 5 contains 3 Bedrooms, Sitting Room, Kitchen and Scullery; outside, W.C. Let to Mr. E. Pritchard at 5/6 per week. The piece of garden ground at the side of No. 5 is let with Cottages Nos. 3, 4 and 5.

The whole thus produces a rental of

### Per £71 : 10s. : 0d. Annum.

Landlord paying Rates and Taxes.

### LOT 2.

## The most attractive Freehold Corner Site

Having long Frontages to Pinner Road and Watford Heath,

AND COMPRISING

### THE FARMHOUSE AND BUILDINGS

KNOWN AS

## "Watford Heath Farm."

The House, which is brick built, rough-cast and tiled, contains 3 Bedrooms, Dining Room, 13ft. by 10ft. 6in.; Sitting Room adjoining, 12ft. by 10ft. 6in.; Kitchen, with Range, Scullery, large Store Room Dairy, Coalshed, and outside W.C. There is an excellent well-stocked Garden. Water and Gas are laid on, and the drainage is connected to the main sewer.

The Buildings comprise brick, timber and slated Cart Shed; timber and slated Granary; timber and tiled range of Cowhouses for 27 cows, converted from old barn, with grain pit, etc.; a brick and corrugated iron range of Cowhouse and Henhouse, and a timber and tiled range of three Pigsties.

The whole comprises an area of about

### 0a. : 3r. : 11p.

and is let to Mr. H. J. Smith till 29th September next, at which date possession will be given.

In the course of widening the Council are to rebuild the boundary wall and make good any of the Cart Shed.

Part of Sedgwick, Weall & Beck's sales particulars for the sale of Watford Heath Farm and the group of cottages on the opposite side of Pinner Rd, including the former Watford Heath School, dated 8 July 1914. The sale was actually postponed until after WW I.

# OXHEY IN PICTURES

Oxhey Hall, dating from the early sixteenth century, (Grade II★ listed building) is built on an ancient site and was recorded as a moated house as early as the twelfth century. It was the property of St Albans Abbey and was held by military service on an inheritable tenancy by its occupiers until the Dissolution of the Monasteries (1536-39) (Early photograph).

Oxhey Hall, little changed (Autumn 2000).

14 Chalk Hill (Grade II listed building) now the property of Alan Luto who has preserved and restored the structure. It is a three bay, two storeyed timber-framed house with later stucco walls and sash windows. The earliest part of the building dates from the seventeenth century.

No 14 viewed from Chalk Hill, the origin of the broken statues in the flint retaining wall (now largely covered with creeper) is uncertain – local legend has it that they came from Oxhey Place, Cassiobury House or even Bushey churchyard memorials!

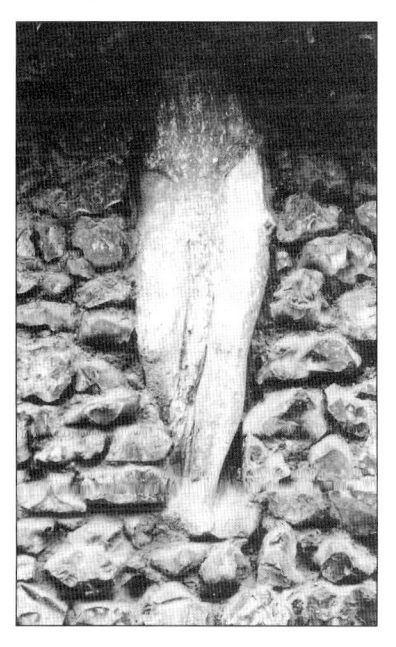

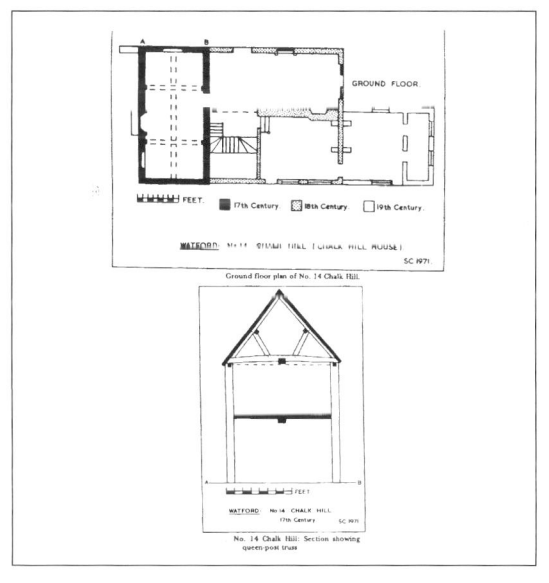

Ground plan and section of 14 Chalk Hill.

Oxhey Place, from an Oldfield Print. This building superseded an older mansion known as St Cleeres or St Clowes and was built in 1688. It was demolished in 1799 for a more modern building. From 1604 the estate was owned by Sir James Altham who built the present Oxhey Chapel in 1612. It had various other owners notably the Heydon family until, in 1866, it was purchased by the Rt. Hon. William Henry Smith, owner of the chain of bookshops which bears his name, W. H. Smith. He sold Oxhey Place to Thomas Blackwell (of Crosse & Blackwell) in 1877. His son, also Thomas Blackwell, died in 1944 and the estate was compulsorily purchased by the then L.C.C. The house was burned down by vandals in 1955.

Oxhey Chapel. The Chapel is said by some to have been founded in 790 but the present building dates from 1612 when it was rebuilt by Sir James Altham. A copy of the Oxhey Charter of 1007 is displayed in the Chapel.

Former Catholic Chapel of the Sacred Heart in Upper Paddock Rd, affectionately known as the 'Tin Tabernacle'. It was demolished in 1959 when its congregation moved to the newly built Church on the London Rd.

Interior of the former Catholic Chapel, the extra chairs at the end of each pew testify to the need for a larger Church.

St Matthews, Oxhey Parish Church, Eastbury Rd (Grade II listed building). The new Parish of Oxhey was constituted in 1879.

Interior of St Matthews.

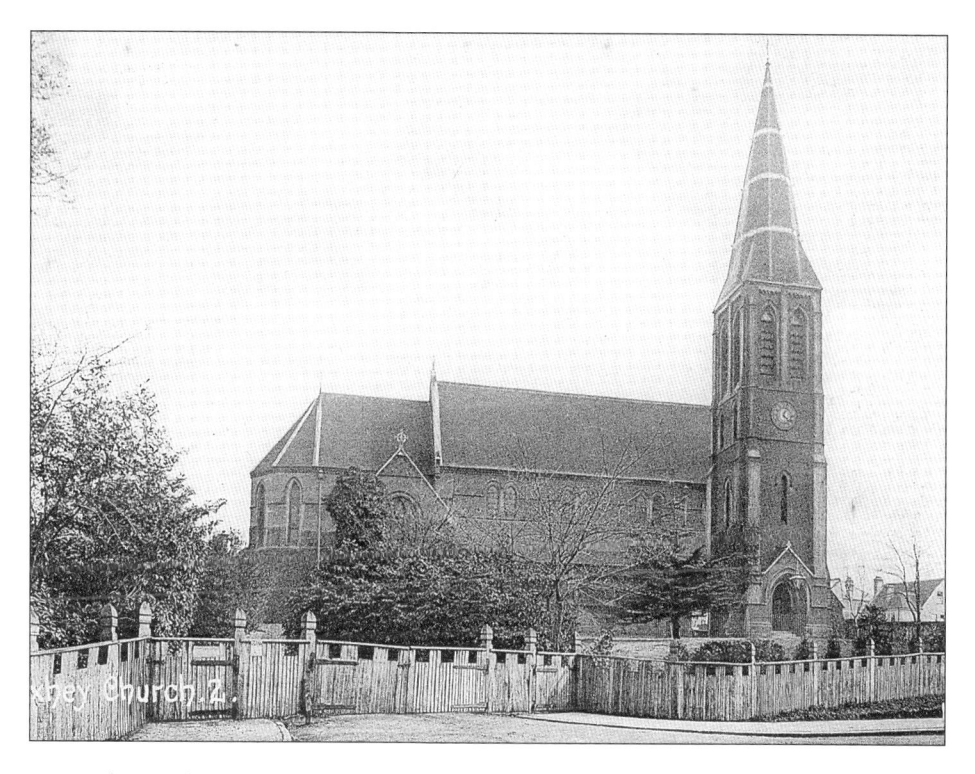

St Matthews Church from the north, c1911.

St Matthews Church, c1950. Trees of Oxhey Park on the left.

Baptist Church, Chalk Hill, before the steps were built so probably before 1890.

Interior of Baptist Church, decorated for Harvest Festival, note the five loaves and two fishes.

Baptist Band of Hope, probably 1905. Venue not known.

Paddock Rd Baptist Church (1999). Founded as Paddock Rd Baptist Chapel in 1911 and known as the Paddock Rd Free Church from 1923 to 1989.

Former Methodist Chapel, Villiers Rd (site now occupied by Nos 45/45a). The structure, of corrugated iron, was purchased from the Plymouth Brethren in 1887. It was moved to become the 'School Room' to the new Methodist Church at the corner of London and King Edward Rd in 1904.

Bushey and Oxhey Methodist Church, consecrated 1904.

The school on Chalk Hill was built in 1879 as a girls' and infants' school by the Bushey School Board. It stood on the corner of Chalk Hill and Aldenham Rd where Faithfield is now.

A re-enactment of a drill display in Victorian times in the playground of 'Oxhey Junior School' by pupils of the 1950s.

An advertisement for 'Kingsfield', a boys' private preparatory school, dated 1936. The small boys with their distinctive yellow caps and shell blazer badges were a familiar sight in Oxhey during the 1930s & 1940s.

Miss Chapman ran a small kindergarten at the Rose Tea Rooms on Watford Heath during the 1930s & 1940s. This picture shows Miss Chapman and Miss Downing greeting two new pupils (Stephen Jaggard and Ann Stones) in 1948.

William Bird stands in the doorway of his father, J W Bird's general store at 33 Capel Rd, c1900. William was killed in WW I.

In about 1905 J. W. Bird moved his shop to 44 Villiers Rd where this picture was taken. Mr Bird became a well-known local character. He died in 1937 (see page 111).

J. W. Bird's premises at 33 Capel Rd were later occupied by J H Nobes. He obviously continued to stock similar merchandise. (Late 1900s.)

E. S. Palmer's grocery store on the corner of Villiers Rd and Capel Rd was established in 1938 and operated until 1996. The premises had previously been a haberdashers and gentlemen's outfitters, Clissolds & Spiers, during the 1920s.

Marshall's provision merchants on the corner of Villiers and Upper Paddock Rd in the 1920s.

R. W. Crawley, electrical and hardware shop occupied the above premises more recently. This picture shows the shop decorated for the wedding of Prince Charles to Lady Diana Spencer on 29 July 1981.

Frank Pargeter and his staff outside his butchers shop (later Dixeys) in Capel Rd, 1930s.

Former slaughterhouse behind Pargeter Butchers just prior to its demolition in 1998. The whole site is now occupied by houses.

Connoisseur Cars, with its proprietor Eric Armstrong, from the forecourt of Bushey Station, 1960s. The site was formerly occupied by a row of three cottages and the Duke of Edinburgh public house. It is currently a Mercedes Benz agent.

W. H. Smith, newsagent c1915. This shop, on the corner of Chalk Hill and Aldenham Rd, was reputed to have been one of the earliest branches of W. H. Smiths in the country. The Rt. Hon. William Henry Smith owned Oxhey Place from 1866-1877 (see page 56).

Within the memory of many middle-aged residents there were at least 15 pubs in Oxhey, now only eight remain (these are indicated by an asterisk in the following list):

  The Arches/Railway Tavern, 1857-1973

*Brookdene Arms (formerly Oxhey Lodge then the Club House of Oxhey Golf Course), c1960s-to date

  Duke of Edinburgh (formerly the Colliers Arms), 1860-1965

*The Happy Hour, Eastbury Rd, 1958-to date

  Haydon Arms, Upper Paddock Rd, c1862 – future uncertain

  King William, 319 Lower High St, kept by the Lonnon family c1840-1959

*Load of Hay, Watford Heath, c1840-to date

  Prince of Wales, Villiers Rd, c1868-1955

*Railway Arms, Pinner Rd, c1858-to date

*Rifle Volunteer, Villiers Rd, c1857-to date

*Royal Oak, Watford Heath, c1860-to date

  Royal Oak, Villiers Rd, prob. c1860-c1960

*The Victoria, Chalk Hill, 1858-to date

*Villiers Arms, Villiers Rd, (date not recorded)

  Wheatsheaf, Lower High St, rebuilt c1750 and in the 1930s, demolished c1994

The Load of Hay, with a load of hay. The present building, with its Welsh slate roof, is thought to date from 1800. It was built originally on 'manorial waste land'.

The Load of Hay in the 1950s.

The Royal Oak, corner of Villiers and Pinner Rd, now a private house, c1930.

Royal Oak, Watford Heath, as in the 1930s. A cottage occupied by Quakers is reputed to have been on this site in 1660, it is also recorded that John Banham built a 'beer house' on a piece of spare land and that Daniel Ford was landlord of a beer house called the Royal Oak in 1819.

Royal Oak, Watford Heath, 1950s.

Villiers Arms, 108 Villiers Rd. A childrens' outing to Burnham Beeches (1920s). Mr Camp, the landlord, is second from the left.

Prince of Wales, 78 Villiers Rd, now a private house.

The Rifle Volunteer, 36 Villiers Rd. Landlord, Mr Webb, standing outside with his dog c1930.

Haydon Arms, Upper Paddock Rd, with George Bennett, landlord from 1910 to the 1930s. This small beer-house was well known as the 'local' for the gardeners from Paddock Rd allotments.

Haydon Arms c1980s. Note stump of tree featured in previous picture still in the pavement. The future of this pub is uncertain at the present time.

The Railway Arms, corner of Aldenham and Pinner Rd. Note Masonic sign over the window. Willie Lonnon (son of the landlord?) is sitting on the right in the carriage, c1890s.

Joe Lonnon, landlord of the Railway Arms, c1890s-1910. His family also kept the King William in the Lower High St.

Former Railway Tavern (later The Arches), Chalk Hill opposite Bushey Arches. Lucketts kept this 'house' for over 90 years. They also hired out horses and carriages; the horses were stabled in fields at the side of the railway embankment behind Aldenham Rd and the carriages housed under the Arch now in the centre of the traffic roundabout. Horse-drawn carriages were replaced in due course by the taxi firm which continues to operate. The Luckett family also ran a local garage and a dairy in Capel Rd. The Arches pub was demolished in 1973 to make way for the new roundabout.

One of Luckett's carriages outside the Railway Tavern. August 1908.

The Victoria (note this is named after a form of carriage not the famous Queen) on the corner of Chalk Hill and Aldenham Rd. c1930.

The 'old' Wheatsheaf, Lower High St c1912. Originally a 'low building' it was rebuilt in c1750 near the Toll House. 'Strolling players', including Henry Irving are reputed to have performed in the garden at the rear. In 1885 a small group of Wesleyan Methodists met in the loft in one of the outbuildings until they acquired their own Chapel in Villiers Rd in 1887 (see page 62).

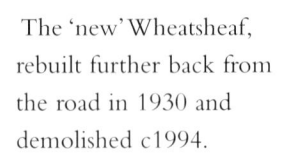

The 'new' Wheatsheaf, rebuilt further back from the road in 1930 and demolished c1994.

Wheatsheaf Cottages stood in a small street called Wheatsheaf Orchard which ran towards the Colne near the junction between the Lower High St and Eastbury Rd. It is not recorded after 1926 and now seems to have been forgotten.

## Chapter 4

# Transport

ALTHOUGH THE FLINT tools, ancient documents and certain seventeenth century buildings confer a respectably long history on Oxhey it must be admitted that the most important piece of paper in the development of the area was the 1833 London and Birmingham Railway Act. It was to the railway that Victorian Oxhey owed its prosperity and, as a home for many commuters, it is the railway that continues to provide Oxhey with much of its living.

The route along which the railway was constructed necessitated a series of cuttings with high bridges across the line and viaducts to carry the railway across low ground. Vast numbers of bricks were needed for these structures and they could be produced locally (see page 14). The elegance of these bridges and the excellence of the brickwork are something of which Oxhey may be proud. Bushey Arches (Grade II listed building) was built by Robert Stevenson and comprises a brick viaduct of five arches each with a 43 ft span and cost £9,700 to build, their total length is 370 ft. One of the Arches spans the London Road and this had to be oblique in order to meet the legal requirement that the line of the turnpike be preserved.

Road traffic on the roundabout through the Arches, (New Year's Day 2000).

Further up the line, behind Oxhey Avenue and beyond, the railway goes into a cutting and it was here, in the days of steam, that water troughs (supplied from wells near the site of the present Bromet School) provided water for the engines. They also made an excellent subject for enthusiastic railway photographers and we make no apology for including a selection of their pictures in this collection.

The growth of road traffic poses a major problem to Oxhey at the present time. Its narrow Victorian streets have become saturated, with either moving or parked vehicles. A way needs to be found to preserve the village's character and yet enable traffic to circulate.

Nineteenth century drawing of Bushey Arches and the London Rd Turnpike from the level of the railway. The high bridge in the distance now carries Oxhey Rd, it comprises three arches and is amongst the highest on the line being 35 ft from parapet to rail level. Watford Heath is in the top left of the picture.

The Turnpike post just below the Arches, marks the position of the old toll gate. Sparrows Herne Trust was the syndicate responsible for maintaining the road from the Arches to the Alpine in exchange for the right to collect tolls from road users. The Trust is thought to have functioned from 1762 to 1872. Originally the road rose more steeply from the Colne up to Crooklog, Bushey but in 1810 the Trust made a deep cutting through Chalk Hill to smooth its irregular gradient.

# OXHEY IN PICTURES

A rather idyllic view of the Arches and Toll Gate in the late 1830s from what is now Eastbury Rd.

THE OLD TOLL GATE, BUSHEY ARCHES. REMOVED 1ST JULY, 1872.

Probably a more realistic view of the Toll Gate – exact date not known.

Artist William Sharp Snr.'s view through the Arches from Chalk Hill – after 1840.

Repairs to the road at Chalk Hill being undertaken at a fairly leisurely pace, 1920s.

One of Luckett's hire carriages beneath the Arches. Luckett's drivers wore top hats in the winter and straw hats during the summer (see page 77).

Luckett's ostlers cleaning a carriage under the Arches.

Horse drawn cab waiting outside Bushey Station.

Bushey Station platform with part of Station Master's house, July 1867 (subsequently demolished).

# OXHEY IN PICTURES

Bushey Station forecourt and Station Master's house, probably also 1867.

Horsedrawn and motorised cabs near lift at Eastbury Rd entrance to Bushey Station.

Postcard identifies this as *Oxhey* and Bushey Station showing the Railway Arms and the Duke of Edinburgh (formerly the Colliers Arms) on the opposite corner. Probably 1930s.

Freshwater Estate Agents Office, Bushey and Oxhey Station. Similar small buildings housed Charringtons and other coal merchants who supplied local householders from the station goods yard.

The goods yard at Bushey Station from which coal was transported by horse and cart down the old 'Coal Wharf' and under the Arches to supply the High St Gasworks.

The unusual occurrence of a snowstorm in late April 1908 is commemorated in this photograph from Pinner Rd.

THE L. & N. W. RLY. SCOTCH EXPRESS (Picking up Water).

A Scots express double header picking up water from the troughs in the Oxhey cutting. The leading locomotive is (for the benefit of any railway buffs) either an N15 2-4-0 Precedent Class, built between 1887-1901 (the last example was withdrawn 1934), or an N16 2-4-0 Whitworth Class (1889-1906), withdrawn in 1932. Both were designed by Francis Webb. There is insufficient detail on the trailing loco for precise identification.

Linear maps showing items of interest to passengers were a common adjunct to journeys up to the 1940s. This early 'Travelling Chart' or Iron Road Book, which illustrated features along either side of the railway between Euston and New Street, Birmingham, probably dates from the mid-nineteenth century.

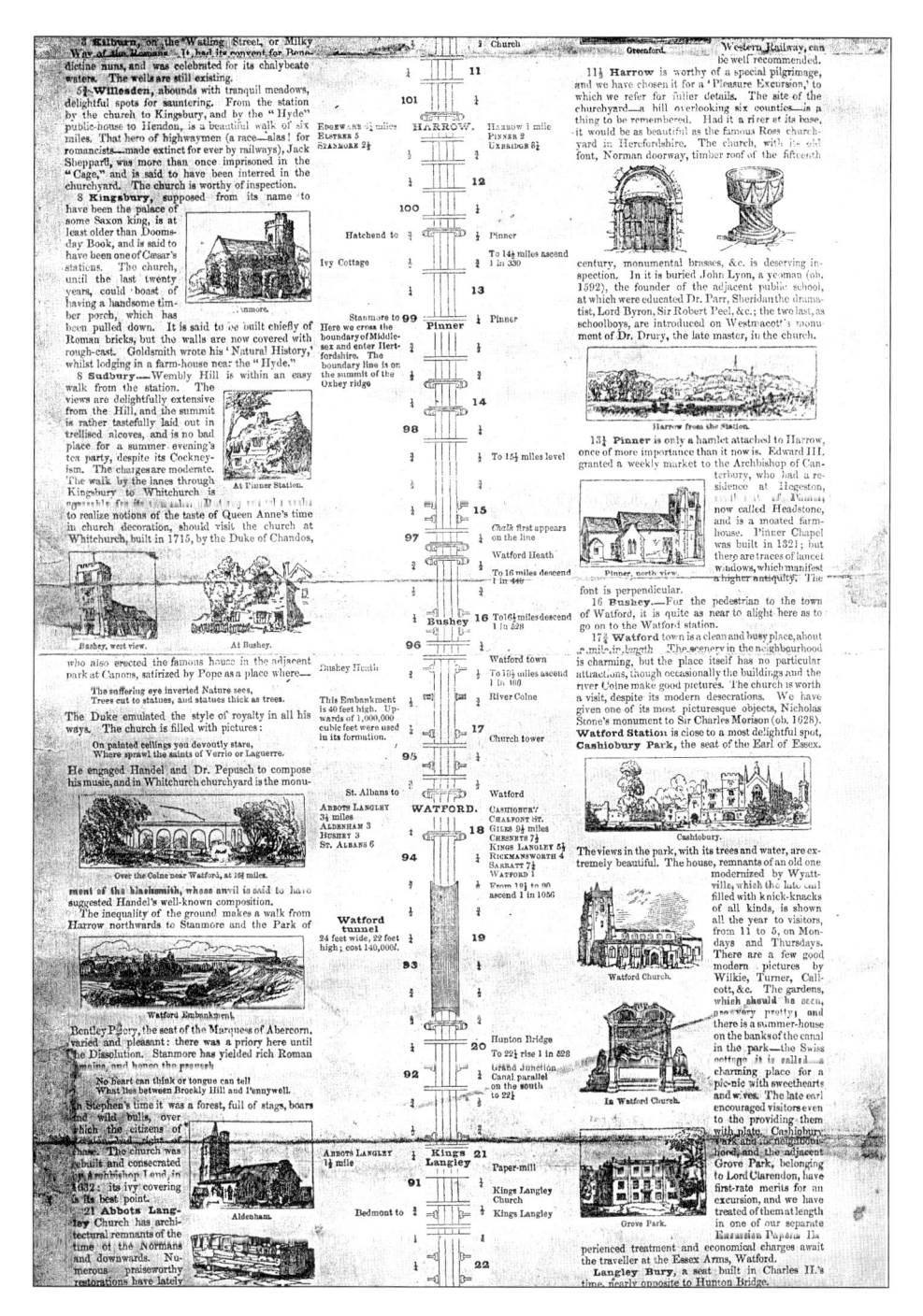

Section of the 'Travelling Chart' covering the line between Harrow and Kings Langley and centred on the Oxhey area.

Locomotive passing under footbridge between Watford Heath and The Pathway heading south. Locomotive an N30 4-4-0 Precursor Class (1904-1907) last withdrawn 1949. Designed by George Whale.

Early commuter train to the City passing under the Oxhey Rd High Bridge at the water troughs. Locomotive either an N12 0-6-2T 'Coal Tank' (1881-1890), withdrawn in 1958, or N25 0-6-2T (1898-1902), withdrawn in 1953. Both designed by Francis Webb.

# OXHEY IN PICTURES

Oxhey cutting and water troughs, train passing under Oxhey Rd High Bridge. Locomotive N34 4-6-0 Experiment Class, (1905-1910) withdrawn in 1935. Designed by George Whale.

Train taking water as it passes under the Watford Heath to The Pathway footbridge. Locomotive probably a 4-4-0 3-cylinder compound, however several similar Classes were designed by Francis Webb in the 1880s.

OXHEY IN PICTURES

**No 27     L.M.S. "ROYAL SCOT" AT BUSHEY ON ROUTE FOR SCOTLAND.**
The Royal Scot, which connects London with Glasgow and Edinburgh in 7 hours, earned fame in Continents by its visit to the Chicago Exhibition in 1933 when it was inspected by 3,021,601 people, and ran no less than 11,194 miles over American and Canadian Railways.

LMS Royal Scot passing under Oxhey Rd High Bridge heading north. Locomotive is the unrebuilt 4-6-0 Royal Scot Class 'Welch Regiment' built before WW II.

Express overtaking a slow train in Oxhey Cutting at water troughs near Oxhey Rd High Bridge. 'Local' loco possibly a N28 4-4-0 Benbow Class compound (1903-c1906) class rebuilt from 1908 onwards. Express loco N10 0-6-0 Cauliflower Class (1880-1902). Withdrawn 1955. Both designed by Francis Webb.

The name of Bushey & Oxhey Station being painted out early in WW II in order to confuse any invaders.

Bushey & Oxhey Station regularly won the 'Best Kept Station' competition after WW II. This shows Platform 1 complete with its garden in June 1953.

'Underneath the Arches' rare view of road traffic through the railway during an overhaul in 1963.

302 Bus at its Watford Heath terminus, 1950s.

Oxhey in Pictures

≈ Chapter 5 ≈

# People and Events

THIS CHAPTER, AS its name suggests, focuses on Oxhey people but also includes the major events which affected both local lives (or were the excuse for group photographs) and, occasionally, the buildings related to those people or events. It begins with the two World Wars and records the sacrifices which Oxhey made in the past and how these continue to be commemorated. This is followed by brief biographies of some notable former residents and their achievements. Finally, roughly in chronological order, pictures of Oxhey people celebrating both national or very local events bringing the record up to date to the year 2000.

THE CHILDREN OF OXHEY CONTINUE TO BE ENCOURAGED TO CULTIVATE THE LAND.

Sunday school children from St Matthews are members of a gardening club, 1900s.

Oxhey Infants, Reception Class, 'helping' to plant a mulberry tree in Oxhey Orchard, 2000.

## Rolls of Honour:
### Listing those Oxhey men lost in the two World Wars, 1914-1918 & 1939-1945

Several local churches and chapels have kept the poignant memory of those killed during World War I by maintaining a Roll of Honour. In particular St Matthews, Oxhey's Parish Church, decided to erect a temporary wooden cross in its churchyard to commemorate 'those 38 Oxhey men who had already given their lives' as early as 1916. Names continued to be added to this memorial until June 1919 when a permanent memorial was erected. The temporary wooden cross was moved to Watford Heath in 1920 where it later fell into disrepair and was removed by the Council in 1951. It is likely that the St Matthews monument was intended to commemorate all those residents of the parish of whatever denomination who lost their lives. However existing Rolls of Honour in other churches and chapels include some additional names. These have all been included in the list below and their churches indicated. Sadly it has proved impossible to trace the Roll of Honour formerly preserved in the Sacred Heart Catholic Church, Upper Paddock Road, until the Church moved to its new building in London Road, Bushey. It is hoped that those names were recorded with the others on the 'Oxhey Parish' memorial.

It has also proved difficult to trace the names of those who gave their lives during the 1939-1945 War. Only the Bushey and Oxhey Methodist Church has been able to provide a list.

### Oxhey Roll of Honour 1914-1918

| | | | | |
|---|---|---|---|---|
| ABBOT, E. | BROWN, F. H. + | EVANS, A. | HOOPER, R. M. + | MORGAN, H. H. ** |
| ABBOT, J. | BUNNAGE, W. | EVANS, D. | HORWOOD, H. J. | NEVILLE, F. C. * |
| ALEXANDER, C. J. | BUTLIN, S. F. | EVANS, W. | IBBOTT, B. C. * | NORTH, S. E. + |
| AHFORTH, W. R. | CHATFIELD, R. F. | EVERETT, C. | IBBOTT, A. D. * | NORTH, W. V. + |
| ATKINS, B. | CHILDS, C. + | EYDEN, R. | JEFFERY, G. L. S. | NYE, A. + |
| AYLING, E. S. | CLARK, W. A. | FIELD, G. + | JEFFERY, J. | PALMER, A. |
| BARNARD, A. H. B. + | COLE, C. C. | FIELD, J. + | JOCKMAN, W. + | PAMMENT, J. |
| BATCHELOR, H. W. ** | COLLINS, F. + | FOUNTAIN, F. | JONES, R. + | PANKHURST, W. J. A. |
| BATCHELOR, J. ** | CONQUEST, L. + | FROST, A. H. ** | KING, J. + | PARKER, G. W. |
| BEAL, A. R. G. | CROFT, C. E. | FROST, F. W. | KNIGHT, A. F. | PREWETT, B. |
| BEAUMONT, G. + | CROUCHER, W. | GATES, A. J. | LAILEY, E. L. | PUGHE, C. R. |
| BEEVOR, T. E. | DAVEY, D. | GORDON, R. | LE MESURIER, N. | PURSSELL, A. J. ** |
| BINYON, H. H. | DEAYTON, G. T. | GROVES, L. | LOVEDAY, F. G. * | RALPH, W. |
| BIRCH, A. | DEBEGER, G. + | HALLIMOND, W. | LOVELOCK, G. V. | RIDDLE, N.; DCM. |
| BIRCH, H. F. ** | DILKS, W. | HANSFORD, F. E. | MACDONALD, J. | ROGERS, J. C. |
| BIRD, W. M. ** | DOCKER, A. E. + | HART, F. | MARTIN, F. | ROE, L. J. + |
| BLIGHT, H. V.; MC. ** | DRAKE, E. ** | HART, W. | MILLER, J. M. | SEABROOK, W. J. |
| BORRETT, H. G. | DRAKE, H. G. ** | HEADY, H. W. + | MILLS, G. | SELWAY, S. J. |
| BOX, W. + | DUDLEY, N. M. C. | HEMMING, F. W. E. ** | MOBBS, E. T. + | SHERVINTON, T. M. R. |
| BRANDON, W. J. ** | DUKE, May * | HODAIN, H. | MOFFET, J. F. + | SHERVINTON, W. H. B. |
| BROUGHTON, H. | DYER, E. J. | HODGINS, H. | MOLONY, C. A. | SHIPTON, J. R. |

| | | | |
|---|---|---|---|
| SLEAT, G. S. | STAVERT, R. E. | VALE, C. S. M. | WILKS, P. W. + |
| SLEAT, H. D. | STEWARD, F. L. | WALKER, A. H. | WILSON, A. + |
| SMITH, A. R. | THRESHER, O. | WARNEFORD, A. J.; VC. | WILSON, C. ** |
| SMITH, J. R. G. | TILLIARD, W. | WATSON, C. S. ** | WINFIELD, F. A. |
| SPROAT, I. + | TIMSON, B. C. | WATSON, W. N. ** | WRIGHT, H. |
| STACEY, J. | TINWORTH, A. + | WESTCOTT, R. H. | |
| STAVERT, G. J. | TYERS, R. | WESTON, D. G. * | |

### 1939-1945

| | | | |
|---|---|---|---|
| ASHWORTH, D. + | HEWETT, L. + | HOWARD, R. + | WREN, D. + |

+ BUSHEY & OXHEY METHODIST   ** BUSHEY BAPTIST CHURCH
* PADDOCK ROAD BAPTIST CHAPEL

### WATFORD HEATH MEMORIAL CROSS

The 'temporary' wooden Cross moved from St Matthews Churchyard was adopted by the residents of Watford Heath during the thirty years it spent on the Heath and it became a particular focus during World War II when flowers were regularly laid at its foot, until its subsequent decay and removal in 1951. A further 30 years elapsed before, in the late 1980s the Oxhey Village Environment Group adopted a proposal to replace the old wooden cross at its original site on Watford Heath. A public appeal was launched in 1993 with a target figure of £1,700. The new simple, elegant Cross was dedicated on 8th May 1994 – the forty-ninth anniversary of V.E. Day. A wreath-laying Service of Remembrance, attended by local residents has taken place at this Cross on Remembrance Sunday every November since.

Memorial Cross, Watford Heath.

The late Ted Parrish, RAF, laying a wreath during the Cross's Dedication Service.

OXHEY IN PICTURES

## SUB-FLIGHT LIEUTENANT R. A. J. WARNEFORD VC RNAS

Reginald Warneford was the first military airman to destroy a Zeppelin in the air and was awarded the Victoria Cross by King George V. Although not a native of Oxhey (he was born in India) he returned to be educated in England and stayed with relatives who are understood to have lived in Oxhey Avenue and/or Kingsfield Road. He volunteered for the Royal Naval Air Service and gained his wings in 1915. During a tour of duty in France he was ordered to locate and destroy 3 Zeppelins which had been spotted returning from a night sortie over England. He chased them behind enemy lines destroying one before his engine failed and he force landed. He managed to repair his plane and take off to fly back undetected to his base near Dunkirk.

He was awarded his VC within 36 hours and also received the Cross of a Chevalier de Légion d'Honneur in Paris, but was tragically killed 10 days later.

Warneford's name is commemorated in Oxhey on the memorial Cross in St Matthews churchyard and by a copper plaque in the south aisle of that church. However, more familiar to Oxhey residents is 'Warneford Place'; named for him, off King Edward Road and in which the former Fire Station stood.

Sadly we have been unable to trace a photograph of Reggie Warneford but we do have a picture of the former Fire Station, taken in 1979.

Old Fire Station, Warneford Place (1979).

The Peace Memorial Statues, erected in front of the former Peace Memorial Hospital, Watford, as a gift from the sculptor, Mary Bromet, were unveiled on 21 July 1928. The group was removed to its present position at the side of the Town Hall when the hospital closed.

MARY POWNALL BROMET, ARBS (Born 1863, died 26 March 1937)

In the Watford area Mary Bromet is best remembered for the three bronze figures which she sculpted at her own expense and presented to the Borough as a memorial to those who suffered during WW I. Her reputation as a major sculptor was however far wider; examples of her work were purchased by Queen Mary and remain in Buckingham Palace. She studied under Rodin in Paris and also in Frankfurt and Rome and exhibited at both the Wembley and White City Exhibitions.

Born Mary Pownall at Leigh, Lancs she came to live in Oxhey on her marriage to Alfred Bromet, a barrister of the Inner Temple, in 1902. Alfred Bromet house-hunted on behalf of his bride-to-be selecting a property near to the artists' colony in Bushey, which had grown up around Sir Hubert von Herkomer, for her benefit. The couple settled happily in Lime Lodge, Heath

Mary Bromet, portrait taken in old age.

Rd, where they were to spend the rest of their lives. Lime Lodge was a gracious, two-storey house with a spacious studio, screened from the road by the lime trees which gave it its name. The Bromets loved their 3-acre garden in which many charity and Conservative functions took place. Alfred Bromet was Chairman of the Oxhey Conservative and Unionist Association and of the Directors of Oxhey Golf Club and an influential figure locally.

The houses in Lime Close and on the south of Heath Rd now cover the site of their house and garden. Mrs Bromet recorded in her autobiography ('Response') her sadness when, in 1913, Oxhey Avenue was built up curtailing her view of Oxhey Woods. Following WW I when funds were being raised for Watford's Peace Memorial Hospital, Mrs Bromet offered to create a memorial for the town. A public appeal was launched to cover the £800 required for its casting and emplacement on a plinth. This amount was quickly achieved, the final donation to reach this target being 14/- from 'the employees of George Luckett'.

Mary Bromet frequently used Oxhey 'locals' as her models and was regarded with great pride and affection in the Village. She died in February 1937 aged 74 after a long illness.

Mary Bromet in the garden of her home, Lime Lodge, Heath Rd, probably c1905.

## OXHEY IN WARTIME 1939-1945

Oxhey itself, despite its proximity to the railway, suffered only minor bomb damage, and one flying bomb in a field near Oxhey Lane (26 June 1944), during World War II and its Victorian Terraces and inter-war houses survived largely unscathed. Pill-boxes were built in Oxhey Park and elsewhere, barbed wire entanglements appeared and all railings and fence-chains were collected – improbably enough for 'constructing Spitfires'. Younger men and women were called up and the older ones became fire watchers, members of the L D V (later the Home Guard) or Air Raid Wardens. There was an Air Raid Wardens Post (H24) in the grounds of Fir Bank House near the 'Piggeries'.

Early in the War Watford Borough Council announced its intention to provide a scheme to collect food scraps from households (separately from the normal refuse collection). These scraps would be boiled up and fed to the pigs on the Corporation's Holywell Farm. In due course dustbins appeared in Oxhey streets, normally chained to lamp-posts, for these household scraps. It is unclear whether Oxhey's scraps were initially collected by the Council or whether they were 'rustled' from the start by local Pig Club members to feed the two or three porkers housed in a small brick building where Field End Close now stands. Certainly all the Talbot Avenue scraps went to 'our' Pig Club and when an animal was slaughtered, although a proportion of the meat had to go to the Government, members of the Club were allowed to share out the remainder for their own use. Mr Duke of Oxhey Street was in day-to-day charge of the pigs and as 'best friend' of his grand-daughter, Christine Cooling was in the privileged position of being allowed to help feed the pigs and lean over their sties to scratch their backs. Back-yard poultry and rabbits were also a feature of local gardens to help eke out the 'rations'.

'Air Raid Precautions', the Anderson Shelter at Mr Laws Nursery, Upper Paddock Rd, c1940.

Former 'Piggeries' near the present Field End Close (1980).

## Reverend Newton Price (1834-1907) and The Watford Heath Cookery School

Reverend Newton Price was a true Victorian philanthropist as concerned for the physical as with the spiritual welfare of his parishioners. Although now largely forgotten Oxhey owes him a tremendous debt since, to a large extent, it owes its separate identity to him.

Newton Price came to Watford in 1867 following his ordination and, in 1872 was appointed chaplain of Oxhey Chapel by the Rt. Hon. W. H. Smith of Oxhey Place. He realised that the growing population of what was then 'New Bushey' needed a parish and church of its own and he campaigned long and hard for this against strong opposition from the incumbents of both Watford and Bushey Parishes. By 1879 he achieved his aim and, largely through his efforts, money was raised to build a new parish church and the District and Parish of Oxhey came into being.

Reverend Price lived with his wife, Hannah, and their five children at the then Vicarage on Chalk Hill. He had been a headmaster in Ireland before he took holy orders and was a life-long campaigner for improvements in education at all levels. There had been an elementary school at Watford Heath from 1854 but by 1872 it had closed. He was the moving force behind its reopening as a mixed Church of England School for about 60 pupils in 1873. Although he was primarily concerned that the '3 Rs' were taught he saw clearly that the well-being of the poorer families in his parish would be improved by ensuring they enjoyed an adequate if economical diet and understood the basis of good nutrition. To this end a purpose built kitchen was constructed in the school playground (now 5 Watford Heath) its cost of £100 being donated by William Eley of Oxhey Grange. Thus Watford Heath School became the first elementary school in the country to teach practical cookery to girls. The cooking was done on a simple kitchen range so that pupils learned to cook under the same conditions they had at home. His aim was 'not to train cooks for rich men's houses but managers for poor men's homes … to teach them economy, ingenuity and cleanliness'. Watford Heath School was closed in 1881 when its pupils were transferred to the new school on Chalk Hill where cookery continued to be taught.

Newton Price played a pivotal role in the creation of the public library and the School of Science and Art in Queens Rd, Watford, in founding the Watford School of

Reverend Newton Price, 1834-1907.

Music and University Extension Lectures were started at his instigation. Deeply interested in the history of Oxhey he translated the Oxhey Charter, which had been discovered in Ireland. The original is now in the Bodleian Library but a copy is displayed in Oxhey Chapel and provides the Frontispiece for this book.

He continued to serve as Vicar of Oxhey until his death in 1907 aged 73.

Former Watford Heath School, main school building now Nos 3 & 4 on the right and the former kitchen (No 5) on the left (c1900).

'Special' menu served by the cookery school to the 'Youths' Guild Supper' as recorded in the Kitchen Journal for 19 April 1877.

103

## Oxhey in Pictures

### Oxhey Golf Course (1912-1946)

During the 1920s & 30s Oxhey was probably more widely known for its famous golf course and its legendary professional, Edward (Ted) Ray, than for any other feature. The course, designed by Harry Varden, was 6,539 yds long for a scratch score of 75 strokes. It occupied an area bounded by the railway to the east, Oxhey Woods to the south and by Hampermill Lane. The Club was founded in 1910 by the Blackwell family, of Crosse & Blackwell fame, who then occupied Oxhey Place which was at the S.E. corner of the Course. The Course opened in 1912 and by 1914 Carpenders 'Halt' had been built to provide golfers with direct access by train from London and Watford.

'Ted' Ray, Club Professional 1912-1940, won the British Open Championship in 1912, the American Open in 1920 and captained the British Ryder Cup Team in 1927. The Course often hosted the National News of the World Tournament and was a frequent contender for the British Open.

The use of the course by trespassing non-members became such a problem that (on the principle that 'if you can't beat 'em let 'em join) the Oxhey Artisan Golf Club was formed, its membership restricted to local artisans. A detailed description of the Course by the well-known golf writer, Bernard Darwin, in 1934, is extravagant in its praise. At that time Alfred Bromet was Chairman of the Board of Directors (the rest were all Blackwells!) of the flourishing Club.

'Ted' Ray, British Open Champion, 1912 and American Open Champion 1920, was Oxhey Golf Club's Professional from 1912-1940.

Oxhey Golf Club House formerly Oxhey Lodge, now the Brookdene Arms.

## Oxhey in Pictures

Sadly in 1943 T. A. W. Blackwell, Club President, heir to the Blackwell Estate and a lieutenant in the Artillery, was killed when the breech blew off his gun. The Blackwell Estate was compulsorily purchased to provide London 'overspill' housing in 1945 and was developed to become South Oxhey. Oxhey Place was burnt down by vandals in 1955. Oxhey Golf Club itself was wound up in 1946. Its last professional was Frank Forge, who had been with the Club for over 40 years. The Club House eventually became the Brookdene Arms but much of the old course remains today as open space occupied by sports fields, a golf driving range and parkland.

Cricket was always traditional (c.f. the MCC) and this team retained its name of 'New Bushey' in 1900 although it played at Watford Heath. The only team member we can name is Mr Wolfe, Club Secretary, second on the left wearing a straw boater.

Paddock Rd Free Church, first outing 3rd July 1912.

Wedding group for the marriage of Percy Jaggard to Sarah Featherby, August 1909, one of the earliest marriages at the Wesleyan Methodist Church in King Edward Rd.

## Paddock Rd Free Church – First Outing – 3rd July 1912

*Top row ( L to R):* Arthur Alexander, Ethel Nash (Mrs Harold Ibbott), Rosie Foster (Mrs Bernard Almond), Frank Jefferys, Clara Jefferys (Mrs R Ellis), Thomas Nash, Gertie Wilkes (Mrs Tom Wolfe), Archie Maddox. *Second Row:* Thomas Wolfe, Charles Duke, Harold Ibbott, Ted Leader, Dorothy Wolfe, Jessie Jefferys (Mrs C Flitton), Mrs Wolfe (Tom's Mother). *Third Row:* Edward Leader, Mrs Gertrude Leader, Mrs Jessie Willis, Thomas Willis, Bernard Almond, Lilian Almond, Christopher Knowles, Grace Ibbott, Arthur Ibbott, Alice Wolfe, Cissie Wilkes, Sam Nash. *Fourth Row:* Mrs Jefferys, Emma Jefferys, Mrs Annie Woodward, Mrs Sam Nash, Ada Capern, George Wilkes, Mrs Shelton, Mrs Victoria Ibbott, Mrs Florence Duke. *Bottom Row:* Dorothy Leader (Mrs Seabrooke), Claude Ibbott, Roberta Woodward, May Duke★, Gertrude Leader, Eva Willis (Mrs Claude Ibbott).

★ The only woman recorded on the 1914-18 Roll of Honour.

## Keyser Hall

Former Baptist Chapel, Lower Paddock Rd. This was purchased in 1893 by Mr C. E. Keyser of Merry Hill House and let on a 21 year repairing lease as a parish hall for Oxhey.

OXHEY IN PICTURES

In 1911 Oxhey Conservative Club took over the lease of this hall as its club premises and later purchased the property naming it 'Keyser Hall'.

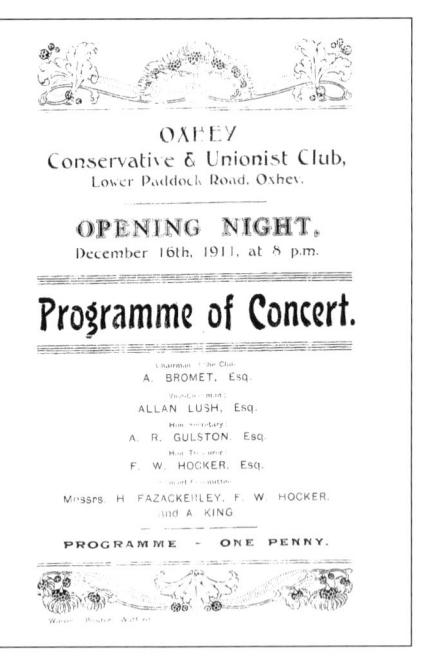

**OXHEY**
Conservative & Unionist Club,
Lower Paddock Road, Oxhey.

**OPENING NIGHT,**
December 16th, 1911, at 8 p.m.

**Programme of Concert.**

Chairman of the Club:
A. BROMET, Esq.
Vice-Chairman:
ALLAN LUSH, Esq.
Hon. Secretary:
A. R. GULSTON, Esq.
Hon. Treasurer:
F. W. HOCKER, Esq.
Sub-Committee:
Messrs. H. FAZACKERLEY, F. W. HOCKER, and A. KING

PROGRAMME — ONE PENNY.

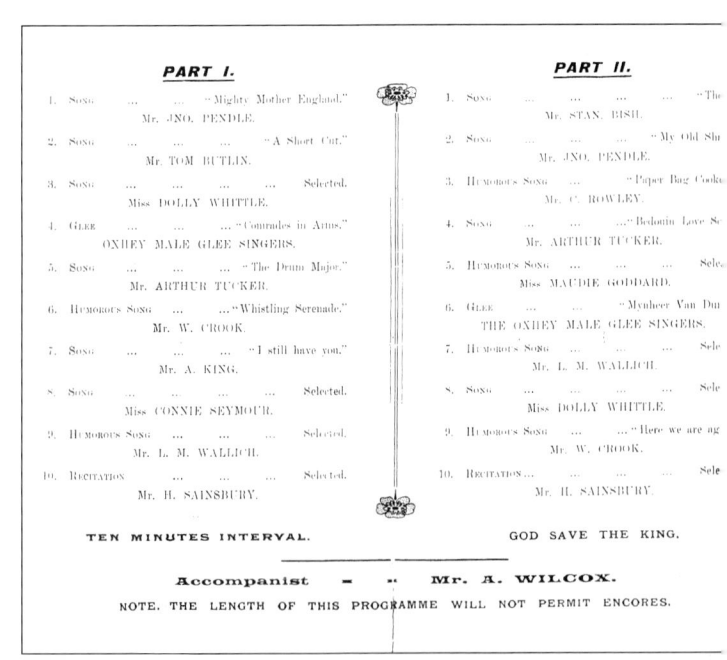

### PART I.

1. Song ... "Mighty Mother England."
   Mr. JNO. PENDLE.
2. Song ... "A Short Cut."
   Mr. TOM BUTLIN.
3. Song ... Selected.
   Miss DOLLY WHITTLE.
4. Glee ... "Comrades in Arms."
   OXHEY MALE GLEE SINGERS.
5. Song ... "The Drum Major."
   Mr. ARTHUR TUCKER.
6. Humorous Song ... "Whistling Serenade."
   Mr. W. CROOK.
7. Song ... "I still have you."
   Mr. A. KING.
8. Song ... Selected.
   Miss CONNIE SEYMOUR.
9. Humorous Song ... Selected.
   Mr. L. M. WALLICH.
10. Recitation ... Selected.
    Mr. H. SAINSBURY.

TEN MINUTES INTERVAL.

### PART II.

1. Song ... "The ..."
   Mr. STAN. BISH.
2. Song ... "My Old Shi..."
   Mr. JNO. PENDLE.
3. Humorous Song ... "Paper Bag Cooke..."
   Mr. C. ROWLEY.
4. Song ... "Bedouin Love S..."
   Mr. ARTHUR TUCKER.
5. Humorous Song ... Sele...
   Miss MAUDIE GODDARD.
6. Glee ... "Mynheer Van Dui..."
   THE OXHEY MALE GLEE SINGERS.
7. Humorous Song ... Sele...
   Mr. L. M. WALLICH.
8. Song ... Sele...
   Miss DOLLY WHITTLE.
9. Humorous Song ... "Here we are ag..."
   Mr. W. CROOK.
10. Recitation ... Sele...
    Mr. H. SAINSBURY.

GOD SAVE THE KING.

Accompanist — Mr. A. WILCOX.

NOTE. THE LENGTH OF THIS PROGRAMME WILL NOT PERMIT ENCORES.

Programme for the Opening Night Concert of Oxhey Conservative & Unionist Club, 16th December 1911.

The Keyser Hall buildings were extended over the years but in 1953 the part which had been the former Baptist Chapel was gutted by fire. This picture shows the immediate cleaning-up operations in progress.

This 1953 aerial view of Lower Paddock Rd and King Edward Rd shows the Keyser Hall (centre) and its former bowling green. Happily the green continues to be maintained as an open space although the bowling club is long gone.

Mr Birch, one of the earliest residents of Villiers Rd, on his doorstep next to the Villiers Arms in 1905.

William Birch (son of Mr Birch, with the barrel on his shoulder) celebrating his 23rd birthday in 1912 with grooms and other members of Blackwell's estate staff at Oxhey Place.

OXHEY IN PICTURES

Villiers Arms Outing to the Races, 1920.

Mr J. W. Bird, local character and former shopkeeper, in his later years – Villiers Rd 1930s.

111

Mr Dennis Herbert, M.P. for Watford, presents the Borough's Charter to its first Mayor, the Earl of Clarendon, at the Borough boundary at the junction of London Rd and Haydon Rd, 18th October 1922.

The Borough Charter's Procession passing down Chalk Hill en route for Watford Town Hall, 18th October 1922.

Beneath a variable thickness of later clays, sands or pebblebeds much of Oxhey is underlain by Chalk. This is a soft, porous limestone which can be slowly dissolved by the passage of rainwater through the ground, which may result in the growth of underground openings within the Chalk. Under certain conditions these cavities occasionally reach the surface resulting in the sudden appearance of holes at ground level.

One such 'swallow hole' occurred in 1866 along the line of the stream which drained Haydon Pond and marked the boundary between Bushey and Watford. The stream continues to disappear into this depression at the bottom of Attenborough's Fields except under conditions of unusually high rainfall when it reasserts itself. In more recent times such swallow or sink holes have been recorded, e.g. in Kingsfield Rd and behind the former Airflow Works in Oxhey Lane.

How the press reported a swallow hole in Oxhey.

The swallow hole, which developed in Kingsfield Rd in 1963, was measured as 12ft deep by 10ft square.

Watford staged a procession to mark King George V and Queen Mary's Silver Jubilee and it is likely that Henry Glenister's cart, photographed in 1935 by Watford Heath, was decorated to take part.

With the coming of Victory in Europe in June 1945 most local roads held street parties. The three pictured here obviously focussed on decorous party teas for the children. Other roads held night-long celebrations targeted at the adults, featuring bonfires, pianos and beer – there is, perhaps fortunately, no photographic record of these.

VE Day party, King Edward Rd.

# Oxhey in Pictures

VE Day Party, Villiers Rd – outside the former Prince of Wales.

VE Day Party, Upper Paddock Rd – near the Paddock Rd Free Church.

Oxhey Darby & Joan Club, 1950s in Miss Thomas's Garden, Oxhey Rd.

Watford Heath Townswomen's Guild as 'street-sellers' for their fête in the garden of Oxhey Grange, 1950s.

## Coronation Celebrations

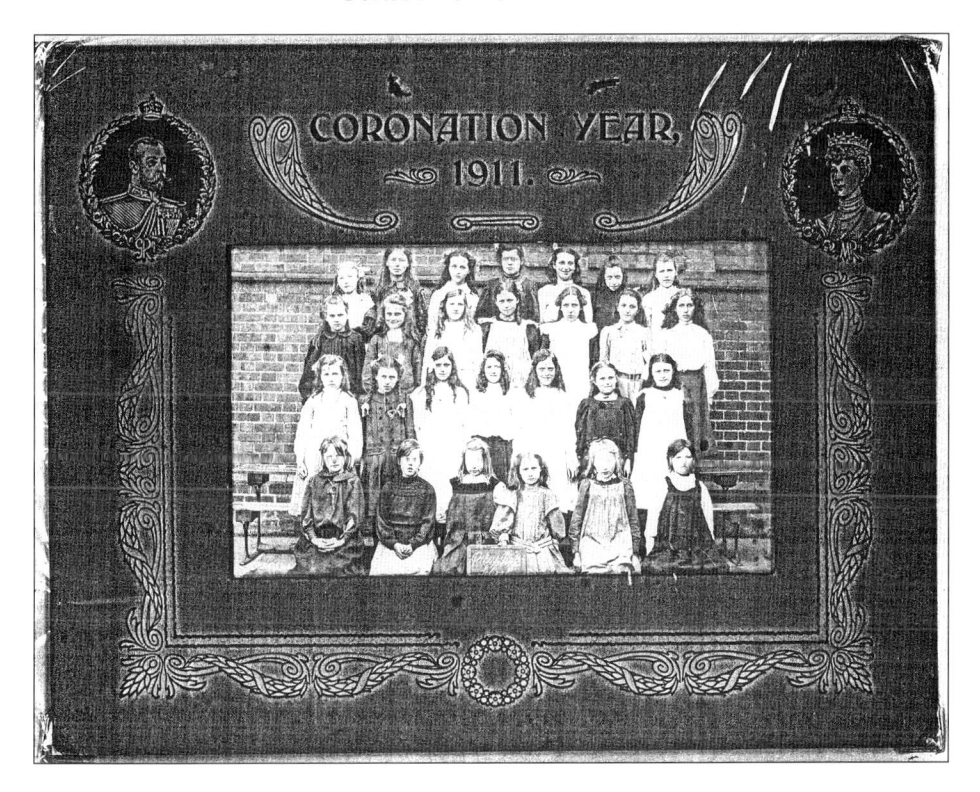

Group from Oxhey Girls' School 'celebrating' the Coronation of King George V & Queen Mary 1911.

Oxhey School celebrated with a fancy dress party and iced cake in 1953.

The Villiers Arms celebrated the Coronation in June 1953 with very special mosaic decorations (made of bottle tops).

Mr Palmer, on his doorstep, decorated his grocery store with the more traditional bunting, flags and photographs of the young Queen.

Villiers Rd held a children's party in the then Parish (now Table) Hall to celebrate the Coronation.

Oxhey children in fancy dress celebrating the Coronation, June 1953.

George Pyne (checked costume) and Frank Marshall (in 'drag') celebrate the Coronation in some style!

Oxhey Village Fayre, on the Green 1976 (Painting by Victor Jones).

## Oxhey in Pictures

Volunteers preparing the site for Oxhey's Orchard on the Paddock Rd Allotments, October 1999.

Oxhey Village Fayre from Park House, 1990s.

# OXHEY VILLAGE ENVIRONMENT GROUP
*Affiliated to The Hertfordshire Conservation Society & The Friends of Attenborough's Fields*

This Book, 'Oxhey in Pictures', has been published by the Oxhey Village Environment Group. The Group, known locally as 'OVEG', was formed over twenty five years ago with the aims of:

- preserving the character of the village
- uniting opposition to any proposal or plan which is out of keeping with its surroundings
- fostering the strong community spirit in the village
- improving the quality of life by every means open to us
- recording the history of life in the area.

Membership is around 600. The OVEG Newsletter is published about every two months with information on Oxhey topics, updates on major planning applications and Oxhey History Sheets.

Our activities include:

- Meetings of local or general interest (with invited speakers) and are usually held in the Bushey & Oxhey Methodist Church
- Meetings open to the public in general on major issues affecting Oxhey
- Occasional outings, including theatre visits
- Special projects such as the restoration of the Watford Heath War Memorial, the publication of Oxhey History Sheets (now in excess of 20) and, of course, this Book
- Each June we hold the Oxhey Village Fayre on Oxhey Green at the top of Lower Paddock Road. Our 25th Fayre was held in 2000.

The annual membership subscription is £1.

For more details about OVEG, or if you wish to join or order additional copies of this Book please contact: OVEG Secretary, 29 Avenue Terrace, Oxhey, Watford WD19 4AP.

## Bibliography

BRAY, M. (1979). 'Oxhey - History of the Parish.' Oxhey Parochial Church Council, Watford.

BALL, A. W. (1973). 'Street and Place Names in Watford.' Watford Borough Council, Watford.

CASTLE, S. (1977). 'Timber-framed buildings in Watford.' Phillimore & Co, London & Chichester.

LONGMAN, G. A. (1977). 'A Corner of England's Garden, 1600-1850.' Watford.

McNAMARA-WRIGHT, R. (1994). 'South Oxhey, A Giant on their Doorstep.'

MONTAGUE-HALL, G. (1938). 'A History of Bushey.' Bushey.

NUNN, J. B. (1987). 'The Book of Watford – A portrait of our town, c1800-1987.' Pageprint (Watford), Watford.

SAUNDERS, W. R. (1931). 'History of Watford.' C. H. Peacock, Watford.

'Watford Observer' Publications on the history of Watford, especially the supplements covering decades in the area's history.

Watford W. E. A. (1987). 'Aspects of nineteenth century Watford.' University of London, London.